Praise for *The Power of the Rosary*

"The Second Vatican Council reminds us of the *consensus fidei*, 'the consensus of belief': the fact that the entire Church — the hierarchy, the religious and the laity, past and present — is called upon to provide a bold witness to the truth and to the transforming power of faith in Jesus Christ. In this book, Gabriel Castillo has dramatically illustrated this aspect of our belief by his own witness — and that of the saints, clergy, and lay people — to the overwhelming power of the Rosary to transform lives and to deepen love for our Savior, Jesus Christ, and His mother, Mary."

— *Fr. Daniel Callam, C. S. B.,*
Holy Rosary Parish, Toronto, Canada

"St. John Paul II famously said the Rosary is destined to bring forth a great harvest of holiness, and this book shows us how. This contemplation of the face of Christ with and through the Blessed Virgin Mary breathes new life into one of the Church's most privileged devotional practices."

— *Most Rev. Steven J. Lopes,* Bishop,
Ordinariate of the Chair of Saint Peter

"Our Lady's invitation to pray the Rosary is an invitation to encounter the mysteries of Christ's life while holding the hand of our mother. Gabriel Castillo's book will ignite in you a new love and zeal for the Rosary. There is no better way to grow in your relationship to Jesus than through Mary!"

— *Mother Amata Veritas Ellenbecker, O. P.,*
Prioress General, Dominican Sisters of Mary,
Mother of the Eucharist, Ann Arbor, Michigan.

"*The Power of the Rosary* is a bold and Spirit-filled rallying cry for our times — solid, clear, and deeply rooted in Marian tradition. I'm honored to endorse this work, which will surely ignite hearts and win souls."

— *Fr. Donald Calloway, M. I. C.,* Author, *Champions of the Rosary*

"Pope Benedict XVI noted that the Rosary is experiencing a new springtime in popular piety. *The Power of the Rosary* stands as a striking example of this movement of grace. This book is both inspirational and formational and, for many hearts, is a sure aid to finding comfort in Mary's motherhood and sanctity through this most anointed of Catholic devotions."

— *Fr. Mark-Mary Ames, C. F. R.,* Director of
Communications, Franciscan Friars of the Renewal

"Gabriel's love for our Blessed Mother and the Holy Rosary is both obvious and contagious. With clarity and devotion, he unpacks the richness of this prayer and how it draws us into deeper communion with the Most Holy Trinity. This book is a beautiful guide for anyone seeking to grow closer to Jesus through Mary."

— *Sr. Mary Mediatrix of All Grace, S. O. L. T.,*
Our Lady of Corpus Christi, Corpus Christi, Texas

"In this marvelous book, Gabriel Castillo refines an ancient practice into a living treasure. He then fashions it into a powerful weapon that links deep spiritual truths to concrete psychological realities. He lays out a step-by-step plan to sainthood along the path of the Rosary. This book is sure to touch the hearts of the young, sinners, parents, and priests. Gabriel gives priceless, timeless, practical tips on how to release the power of the Rosary in your life."

— *Fr. David Michael Moses,* Founder, Pilgrim Rosary

"*The Power of the Rosary* is an invaluable guide to strengthening our union with Christ through Mary. Written from personal experience and faithful practice of the devotions he recommends, Gabriel Castillo has offered a gift to the Church and to families that will promote holiness and help many souls find salvation for many decades to come."

— *Fr. Sebastian Walshe,* O. Praem., Prefect
of Studies, St. Michael's Abbey

"Serving as chaplain for steadfast pilgrims 'in haste' to the Holy House of Loreto during the Holy Year, I can attest that this book can be a loyal companion for your own pilgrimage. Gabriel is unafraid and prophetic for our time, boldly reminding 'all generations' that Mary, as a woman and school of prayer, is the pilgrim's surest way to our Precious Lord."

— Fr. Nicholas M. Divine, C. P., Retreat Master,
Holy Name Passionist Retreat Center, Houston, Texas

"Any lover of Our Lady and her Rosary will find this book to be a great aid and treasure. It is both sublime and practical."

— Fr. Elias Mary Mills, F. I., Retreat Leader and
Missionary, Franciscans of the Immaculate

"Yes! Let the call of this powerful book reach the ends of the earth. Pray the Rosary!"

— Fr. Mark Goring, C. C., Author, *St. Joseph the Protector:
A Nine-Day Preparation for Entrustment to St. Joseph*

"There's no prayer like the Rosary, and there's no one who talks about it like Gabe Castillo. This book packs a powerful punch of information, motivation, and encouragement. Read this, and I promise you will never doubt the power of the Rosary."

— Keith Nester, Author, *The Convert's Guide to Roman
Catholicism* and *Unpacking the Mysteries of the Rosary*

"This is a video in book format, with motivation on every page. If you want to be a saint, you need to pray the Rosary. And if you want to get motivated to pray it, you need to read this book."

— Fr. Matthias M. Sasko, F. I., Author, *Preparation for Total
Consecration to the Immaculate According to Saint Maximilian M. Kolbe*

"Reading this book transformed my devotion to the Rosary. I was badly in need of renewal, but now I have a newfound love for the Rosary and an understanding of its richness for the spiritual life, self-discipline, love for Mary, and intimacy with God. If you desire renewal and a new vision of the Rosary's place as essential for holiness, you must read this book!"

— *Sr. Thomas Aquinas Betlewski,* Dominican Sister of Mary,
Mother of the Eucharist, Ann Arbor, Michigan

"Castillo marshals all the most Marian saints who have ever sung Our Lady's praises, selects their sharpest spiritual weapons, and brings them together in a panoply of inspiration fit for spiritual warfare. Adding his wisdom and personal pastoral experience to theirs, he reminds us just how powerful the Rosary has been throughout the ages to support and, indeed, make efficacious Christ's work for the salvation of souls. This book opens even wider the way for Our Lady so that she can help us all become saints too!"

— *Fr. Ambrose Criste,* O. Praem.,
Norbertine Canon Regular, St. Michael's Abbey

THE POWER OF THE ROSARY

GABRIEL CASTILLO

THE POWER OF THE
ROSARY

SOPHIA INSTITUTE PRESS
Manchester, New Hampshire

Sophia Institute Press
Box 5284, Manchester, NH 03108
1-800-888-9344
www.SophiaInstitute.com

Sophia Institute Press is a registered trademark of Sophia Institute.

paperback ISBN 979-8-88911-394-2

ebook ISBN 979-8-88911-395-9

Library of Congress Control Number: 2025941005

Third printing

Contents

Foreword

I AM THE FOURTH SON of a Pentecostal pastor. I grew up in a family that placed prayer at the very center of life.

Two phrases that were frequently expressed throughout my childhood were: "The family that prays together stays together," and "Prayer is the mightiest force in the world."

My parents didn't just say things like that—they lived them. Each night before bedtime, we would read the Scriptures together as a family. We often focused on the Psalms, basking in the richness of their musical beauty and theological depth. The Psalms were uniquely appealing, especially for us children. They seemed to be singable, prayable, memorable, quotable, understandable, relatable—and, dare I say—livable.

I still remember the surge of hope that entered my soul when I first encountered this special promise in Psalm 1 for those who meditate on the Word of God:

> *And he shall be like a tree planted by the rivers of water*
> *that bringeth forth fruit in season;*
> *his leaf also shall not wither;*
> *and whatsoever he doeth shall prosper.* (v. 3)

As a child, I could never have imagined that those Psalms—and that promise—were an early preparation for Our Lady's Psalter and all the breathtaking promises given to those who meditate on its mysteries. As I once said to my cradle Catholic wife, "I'm never going to become Catholic."

The punchline? I was received into Holy Mother Church on February 20, 2022.

I'm Catholic—and I love it.

My conversion was due in large part to my wife's commitment to praying a five-decade Rosary for me every day for a year.

The Rosary accomplished what arguments and debates could never achieve: it conquered my heart through Our Lady's tenderness.

I am a captive of the Rosary—but thankfully, my story doesn't end there.

While going through RCIA, I began watching videos from Gabriel Castillo about the Blessed Virgin Mary, the Holy Spirit, and the power of praying the full Rosary. His talks took me to the next level. Every word he spoke seemed to be infused with a love for Mary that drew me deeper and deeper into our Blessed Mother's heart. The more I listened, the more I wanted to pray. And the more I prayed, the more I wanted to be consumed by prayer.

Although it seemed impossible, Gabi inspired me to make a commitment to pray all four mysteries—the full 20 decades—every day for a year. My wife, inspired by that example, committed to doing the same. At the end of the year, the verdict was clear: "We can't afford to stop doing this."

Our marriage is being healed and renewed in ways we could never have accomplished on our own. Our love for Jesus is greater than it's ever been. Our desire to serve our parish community just keeps on growing. The grip of habitual vices and nagging sources of discouragment get weaker by the day. Our love for the Holy Mass, for Confession, and for Eucharistic Adoration continues to get the last laugh over my former self who once proclaimed, "I've had enough church."

But my testimony is only one of many. Mary is building an army of Rosary warriors all over the world. And she isn't just building an army—she's gathering her children. She's calling back the lost. She's awakening the hearts of those who were never interested. She's healing the souls of those who thought they were too wounded to go on. She's illuminating minds that once seemed unshakably skeptical. She's liberating those enslaved to addictions and worldly attachments. She's building a global family of children who will share Mama's heart until the whole world is permeated with her love.

This book was written by a man who possesses Mama's heart. Gabriel Castillo is a true child of Mary. He doesn't merely study Mary or speak about Mary—Gabriel loves Mary. And he lives continuously in the assurance of her undying love towards him.

That's why this book is more than informative—it's contagious. When you read his words, you will learn many things, but more importantly, your heart will be inflamed with deeper devotion to Our Lady. This book isn't merely about prayer. It's the product of prayer. And if you're holding this book in your hands, I strongly believe that it's because someone's prayer for you is about to be answered. Our Lady has a special role for you, and this book is the perfect book for helping you to discern that role.

T.K. Coleman
April 4, 2025

THE POWER OF THE ROSARY

Introduction

IN THIS BOOK, YOU will discover a key that unlocks every door in the spiritual life. The Rosary is not just a pious devotion; it is theological gold, a sword forged by God to conquer every battle and overcome every obstacle.

This prayer was created by the hands of the Mother of God to turn ordinary people into saints. When it is prayed well, the Rosary contains in it a profound science that yields an increase in every aspect of life. Because the Rosary is so rich, this book by necessity will touch on a number of profound spiritual topics. On this journey, you will hear the voices and feel the encouragement of the greatest saints and authorities in the Church.

The title was intentionally chosen as a nod to the spiritual classic *The Secret of the Rosary* by St. Louis de Montfort. His book—the greatest Rosary resource available in the twentieth century—played a major role in deepening my love and understanding of the Rosary. However, an updated explanation and defense of the Rosary is needed.

The world and the Church have changed a lot since the 1700s. Humanity has seen major world wars, a sexual revolution, and an exponential rise in technology. The Church has put her stamp of approval on several major Marian apparitions that had the Rosary as a central message. We have also benefited from the wisdom and insights of remarkable saints like St. Alphonsus Liguori, St. Maximilian Kolbe, and St. Padre Pio, as well as the introduction of the Luminous Mysteries by St. John Paul II.

One important note: Everybody is at a different point in the spiritual journey. As you read, take only what applies to you, and cling to the things that resonate. If at any point you feel a call to pray the Rosary, I recommend you mark your spot and then take a moment to skip to the 7th chapter to get valuable tips that will help you pray the Rosary more faithfully. In that chapter, I also give a step-by-step guide on how to implement and persevere in the family Rosary.

The information contained in this book is priceless. Before continuing, I encourage you to say a short prayer to the Holy Spirit. Try to read this with a sense of the presence of Mary. She is with you, and with a prayerful disposition and an open heart, you too will be convicted of the power of the Rosary.

Dear Young People,

God has created you with a plan and a purpose; discovering that plan and living His purpose is the greatest adventure in life. St. Catherine of Sienna said, "If you simply become who God created you to be, you will set the world on fire."[1] This is true, but we can take it even further: God's will for your life is everything!

Living God's will is the key to satisfying the longings of the human heart. Living His will is the secret to sanctity. Living His will is the secret to saving countless souls. Living His will is the secret to unleashing the power of Christ in the world.

The enemy of your soul has set up countless traps for young people. When we are very young, he starts small, for example, by encouraging the question: "What do you want to be when you grow up?" That seems harmless, but it doesn't include the major question of God's will. The questions we should be asking are, "What is God calling me to do? Who is God calling me to be?" From God you have come and to God you must return.

The traps of the devil only get more sophisticated with time. The confusion and perversion that opposes you is so pervasive that it can only be avoided and overcome with the help of God. Being the person God created you to be will require heroic virtue, but as sin abounds, grace abounds all the more.

God has given you a weapon, a tool that is so powerful it ensures victory: the Holy Rosary of the Virgin Mary. If you take up the Rosary as a way of life, you will discover God's will, overcome every obstacle, and become a saint. You might not get canonized, but you will go to Heaven, and you will bring countless souls with you.

Dear Sinners,

Sinners? Who am I talking to? Yes, we are all sinners, but I am speaking to those constantly in mortal sin, anyone that feels like a slave, anyone that feels hopeless, or like a failure, or a lost cause. I have incredible news: There is hope. There is freedom. I promise you liberation. I have seen it. I have lived it.

The Virgin Mary utterly humiliates the devil. So much so that she doesn't just liberate the captives, she turns her new children into liberators of souls. By becoming a child of Mary, you can have a new life in

Christ and enter into His victory—but it is going to cost you. Anybody who wishes to save his life will lose it. But if you offer your life to God, through Mary, you will have freedom and peace.

If you are ensnared in sin, your circumstance is serious and so is the remedy, but Our Lady has a plan for you. The Rosary has never failed to destroy vice in the lives of those who persevere in this devotion. Read that again, with an open heart. Then take Mary's hand, and let her lead you on this journey of transformation and sanctification. I can make these bold promises of freedom and liberation because Mary made them first, and the saints attest to her power over sin. She never fails. You will either leave the sin behind, or you will give up the Rosary. Yes, you will need to take practical steps to overcome addiction and to practice virtue, but you also need spiritual assistance. When confronting mortal sin, there is a spiritual dimension. The devil cannot be defeated by self-help alone. You need the help of the Mother of God. Take up the Rosary.

Dear Parents,

In the history of humanity there has never been a more difficult time to raise children. Think of it. A parent can do everything possible to raise a child right, only to discover that hard work being undone within the very walls in which that child is raised. Because of technology, a child can physically be at home while his mind and heart are somewhere else. Yet despite these obstacles, I tell you, do not be afraid. It is possible to raise holy, happy, and "normal" children, even today!

Perhaps you are heartbroken over your child's loss of faith. I know many parents who converted later in life, whose children don't live the faith. So many parents live with great regret that they didn't do things differently.

Regardless of your situation, Our Lady has a plan for you. Are you willing to fight? It is a battle, but with her you will fight and win. They call us the Church Militant for a reason! We must fight for our children. If we enter into Mary's plan for marriage and the family, we are going to be victorious. Parents, don't wait to finish this book to start praying the Rosary!

Finally, we often think about the things we should or shouldn't do in order to be good parents, but the number one thing we must do to be good parents is be good spouses. In the sacrament of Matrimony, we make a sacramental covenant with God to try to get our spouse to Heaven. This is our vocation. Our salvation and holiness depend on this. The Rosary will help us to become saints in our married love, saints who love with their whole hearts and constantly sacrifice for the sake of the beloved. Be a saint for your spouse. Pray the Rosary for your spouse. How wonderful for a child to be able to look at their mom and dad and say, "Wow. I am so blessed that she is my mom. My dad is literally a saint. Thank you, Jesus." My friends, if you take the content of this book seriously, Our Lady will transform you and your family.

Dear Priests,

Finally, I get to speak to you. I really love you. I wrote this book for you most of all. Our families need holy priests, men of sacrifice and deep prayer. A priest, if he is going to be in the image and likeness of Christ, must be a child of Mary. Our Lady, through the Rosary, will radically transform your ministry. A priest who is a faithful child of the Rosary functions on an entirely different level in ministry.

When a priest prepares for his homilies with Our Lady by praying the Rosary, she puts on his heart what will benefit souls the most. Then, in his delivery of that message, she intercedes with her Spouse, the

Holy Spirit, and the message hits more deeply. His words are like seeds being planted in the soil of his listeners' souls. I am not saying that Our Lady will change your style and that you will start preaching like Fulton Sheen. But when you speak, your words will penetrate. Think of Mother Teresa. She spoke slowly, she was measured, but her words carried a certain weight to them. She spoke with the anointing of the Holy Spirit. She was a true child of Mary, always praying her Rosary. Our Lady will do the same with you, but you must be open.

Our Lady will also help you in the confessional. Recall the life of St. John Vianney. The devil would come and beat him before a big Confession. Why? Because it was the personal prayer life of this priest that was obtaining the grace of conversion. The more you pray, the more Our Lady will draw souls to you. When they come to you, if you are docile to her voice from praying the Rosary, she herself will inspire your counsel in the confessional.

No doubt the Rosary is both simple and theologically profound, and I know you will see how it truly is the key to every facet of the spiritual life. Our Lady in her Rosary will draw close to you. She will make her presence in your life felt in a personal way. Mary loves priests, but you must call upon her constantly. Like Christ, you must draw close to Mary for comfort and counsel. Let her hold you and take care of you. In the mental prayer of your Rosary, you will spend time with her. Standing by her side at the Crucifixion, you will accompany her in sorrows, and in return, she will accompany you always. Trust her. She will help you not just to be a good priest, but a saintly priest. God has chosen you to be a priest at this time in history for a reason; we need you.

Start with the End in Mind

*When the Holy Rosary is said well, it gives Jesus and Mary
more glory and is more meritorious than any other prayer.*

— St. Louis De Montfort[2]

*The Rosary is the most beautiful and the richest of
all prayers to the Virgin Mary; it is the prayer that
touches most the heart of the Mother of God.*

— Pope St. Pius X[3]

*I advise you as earnestly as I can, and even
adjure you not to allow a single day to pass
without reciting the Rosary, which is most
pleasing to God and the Blessed Virgin Mary.*

— St. Francis de Sales[4]

SHORTLY AFTER MY CONVERSION, I would come across
bold claims like the ones above. I accepted them and believed
them, but deep down I thought they were just pious sayings. As I
slowly began to mature in my faith and come to believe that Catholicism was objectively true, I realized that the saints were not just pious
people. Yes, although many were simple and holy, a great number of
them were intellectual giants, Doctors of the Church, and masters
of mystical theology and spirituality. It was these spiritual giants who
were great devotees and champions of the Rosary.

I too have now come to believe in the power and efficacy of
the Rosary, not based on piety but on theology. I am convinced

that truly a greater prayer does not exist. G. K. Chesterton said there were thousands of reasons to be Catholic, and all of them amount to this: It is true.[5]

The same sentiment holds about the Rosary. There are many reasons to pray it, but ultimately only one reason: It is the best. Pope Leo XIII said, "We think the best and most effective way to Mary's favor lies in the Rosary."[6] All the greatest saints agree that the Rosary is theological genius, a master class in spirituality. God willing, you too will be convinced that the Rosary is truly the greatest prayer—not just for Roman Catholics but for everyone.

Part of the reason I was slow to really be convinced of the truth behind these bold claims from the saints was that, when I prayed the Rosary, it didn't always feel good. Among my peers it felt like there was a kind of devotional relativism. They would say things like, "It doesn't really matter how you pray, just as long as you pray." I was confused, and I had questions. If the Rosary is so great, why is it difficult? It doesn't feel like anything is happening. Am I even doing this right? We will examine all of that. Together, we will build your devotion on a solid foundation of truth, so that you will remain steadfast even in dryness and difficulty. We will also explore how to pray the Rosary "well."

First, in order to properly appreciate the Rosary—or any devotion for that matter—and adequately evaluate its power and perfection, we must first examine the goal of the spiritual life. What is the end game? In any aspect of life, if you want to succeed at something—business, fitness, holiness—you must start with the end in mind. Only after examining the goal can we make clear choices about what steps are needed to succeed. Anybody can learn how to pray the Rosary, but if we are going to persevere in this devotion, we must be convicted of the *why* behind it.

THEOSIS: THE GOAL OF THE SPIRITUAL LIFE

The deepest longing of the human heart is true and lasting happiness. God created us with an eternal ache that no earthly thing can satisfy. This ache can be satisfied only by God, who wills to play an intimate and personal role in all of our lives.

Often people turn to religion to heal something or to get a sentimental feeling, but they don't surrender every aspect of their lives to Christ in a personal way. Even within Christianity, some people reduce Christ's saving work to "fire insurance," ensuring they will not be punished in the afterlife. God's plan for salvation is so much more profound than a bargain or an exchange. The intimate union God wants with us is so deep that all through Sacred Scripture the highest analogy used is the union of a married couple who are no longer two but one. St. Paul said, "It is no longer I who live, but it is Christ who lives in me" (Gal. 2:20). St. Peter takes it further: We will "share in the divine nature" (2 Pet. 1:4). St. Athanasius echoes the same: "God became a man so that Man might become like God."[7]

This is essential. The end of Christianity is union with God: to become one with Christ, to resemble Him, to let Him live and love and act through you. Theological terms for this include *theosis*, divinization, deification, and sanctification; in simpler terms: You become holy. God reveals Himself to you, and you become like Him. It sounds like you are losing yourself, but that is the great paradox of Christianity: From death comes life. The more you die to yourself, the more alive you become. And the incredible thing is, the holier you become, the more intensely yourself you become: more alive, more vibrant, more of who you were meant to be.

As you begin this journey of theosis, what will happen is that the grace that God is pouring into your life will begin to pour out into the life of your family. Through you, Christ enters the home, the workplace, the school. Other people see a person fully alive, a person who is happy. To be holy and to be happy are synonymous. Only those who are holy can be truly happy, because to be holy is to discover God's plan and purpose for your life.

The process of becoming holy isn't arbitrary, and your progress cannot be measured by how you feel. So many people are misled and taught to go off feelings. To make decisions based solely on your feelings is a recipe for disaster, because part of the process is striping away self-love and self-will in exchange for God's love and God's will. Christ said, if you wish to be my disciple you must deny yourself (see Matt. 16:24).

What does all this have to do with the Rosary? Everything. You will soon see that in the Rosary there is a stripping away of your self. There is a death and self-denial, but what dies is the worst, most selfish part of ourselves, and what is left is beautiful — and well disposed. We are given the grace to know God's will and the strength to do it. He fills us with His love and divine life. This is why it is so important to understand the Rosary. Starting with the end in mind, being convicted of the theology and intellectual truths, will help you to persevere in the Rosary in times of dryness and desolation.

Theosis, union with God, is becoming a saint. It is the only path to Heaven. Every person in Heaven is a saint, and Heaven is our ultimate purpose. God and His Church decide who will be canonized as examples for the Church, but we should all strive to live lives worthy of emulation. You must strive to become the person God created you to be. To become a saint is a lifelong process of purification of our will, training in virtue, and, most importantly, participating in a divine action. The Rosary will act as a force multiplier in every part of the process of sanctification.

Essential Elements of Holiness

I want to share with you four areas that every one of us must prioritize if we are to become holy. These are not four steps, and they do not take place in any particular order; instead, these are essential elements by which we are conformed to Christ.

1. *The infinite power of God comes to us in the sacraments.*

The most profound means of becoming one with God is the worthy reception of the sacraments. Deification is an act of grace. Jesus' life-giving love is a free gift; we simply need to receive it. Jesus instituted the sacraments specifically to give us the grace necessary to make us partakers of the divine nature. No ordinary human activity can make up for what the sacraments provide. In the sacraments we are brought into contact with the divine power of God.

In Baptism we become temples of the Holy Spirit, true tabernacles of the presence of God, and members of the Body of Christ. We abide in Him, and He in us. In Baptism, we also become true children of God the Father. In and with Christ, we cry out *Abba Father*. We are baptized into the death of Christ, which cost Him everything, but for us it is free. This is the first step in becoming saints.

During the Holy Sacrifice of the Mass, we are made present at the one sacrifice of Christ. We stand at the foot of the Cross with Mary and offer Jesus to the Eternal Father for our salvation, our sanctification, and all of our needs, both spiritual and temporal. It is the Crucifixion of Christ that is the catalyst for our becoming like God. The Holy Sacrifice of the Mass is the most powerful force on earth. When we receive Holy Communion, we receive Jesus Christ whole and entire. The amount of grace that is made available in just one Holy Communion is enough for the salvation and sanctification of the entire world, because in the Holy Eucharist the entire Christ is contained.

In the Eucharist is contained *pure power*. Think of the power of the sun. Humans cannot fathom getting physically close to the sun; we would be annihilated because of the power it contains. Yet in the Holy Eucharist is the God that created every star in the sky. Unimaginable, infinite power is available in the Eucharist. One Holy Communion is enough to make me a saint, to effect perfect divinization, but it doesn't. Why not?

In the Eucharist is contained *pure love*. When Jesus revealed Himself to St. Margaret Mary Alacoque, He showed to her His Heart crowned with thorns and consumed with fire, a true furnace of divine love. Jesus told St. Margaret Mary that He suffered more now in the Holy Eucharist than He suffered during His entire Passion because of the ingratitude of men. He complained that so few people visit Him, that people receive Him carelessly and without love. Churches are locked, and He is a prisoner of love waiting in the tabernacle. His Heart is engulfed with love for men, and yet Jesus is met with indifference and resistance. Why? Why don't we respond to Jesus in the Holy Eucharist with the love that He longs for?

In the sacraments we have the infinite power and infinite love of God, but we only receive grace in proportion to our disposition. Are we open? How do we get closed souls to open? Heaven has given an answer: the Rosary. The Rosary opens our hearts to the graces of the sacraments as no other prayer does.

2. *Mental prayer is a gateway to the spiritual life.*

Of course, prayer is on the list of essentials to a life of union with God, and the most obvious form of prayer is petition. After all, Jesus Himself tells us to ask, to seek, and to knock (see Matt. 7:7–8). It is God's will that we petition Him. It is an act of humility and an act of faith. We must petition, asking Him to help us to open our hearts, to save our souls, to know His will, and to receive Him worthily.

That being said, petition is not the type of prayer that I want to focus on here. The type of prayer that turns ordinary men into saints is called *mental prayer.* Listen to what some of the greatest saints had to say about it:

> St. Alphonsus: "All the saints have become saints by mental prayer. Mental prayer is the blessed furnace in which souls are inflamed with the divine love."[8]

> St. Teresa of Ávila: "He who neglects mental prayer needs not a devil to carry him to Hell, but he brings himself there with his own hands."[9]

> St. Francis de Sales: "[In mental prayer] your whole soul will be filled with Him, you will grow in His likeness.... Listening to His words, watching His actions.... Believe me, ... there is no way to God save through this door."[10]

I bombard you with quotes from Doctors of the Church because many modern audiences have not even heard of mental prayer, and it is truly indispensable. I too was hesitant to accept mental prayer, because I had never heard of it. Honestly, it intimidated me. I didn't think I was smart enough to understand it nor good enough to practice it. I was so wrong. Even little children can understand and practice mental prayer.

It is so monumental; I can only describe it as nuclear power in the spiritual life. When you begin to pray the Rosary using mental prayer, everything changes. You will sense the power and efficacy of prayer and soon be convinced that you can move mountains. We will address the how, what, and why of mental prayer and the Rosary in a later chapter, but for now, I bring it up because without prayerful meditation, you cannot know Christ. Mental prayer is a framework in which you contemplate some aspect of His life, which leads you to a genuine encounter with Him.

Spending time with Christ in some aspect of His ministry changes you. Theosis occurs then and there. You become like Him. According to St. Teresa of Ávila, mental prayer is the gateway to all the higher forms of prayer; and according to St. Alphonsus, God rarely answers those who do not pray in this way. Petitioning Jesus in mental prayer takes on a greater weight. Our Lady, by giving us the Rosary, ensures that we encounter Jesus in mental prayer every day. She gives us a pattern for mental prayer and acts as our guide. Mental prayer in the Rosary changes everything; you will find that with Our Lady the presence of God is magnified in our life, and we leave prayer having a clearer understanding of God's will.

3. *Union with the will of God is the essence of holiness.*

Jesus said it is not those who say "Lord, Lord" who will enter the kingdom of God, but only those who do the will of their heavenly Father (see Matt. 7:21). The will of God — discerning it every day at every moment — this should be our obsession. St. Maximilian Kolbe says that to do the will of God is the essence of holiness. Therefore, the best prayer should help us to love God's will, know His will, and obtain for us the grace to accomplish God's will. When we do God's will, we have peace of soul.

Sacrificing your will to do God's will turns every activity into a prayer. When you wash the dishes, when you wait patiently in a line, when you do even ordinary tasks with love — because they are God's will — these simple actions flood your life and the lives of your loved ones with grace. By embracing God's will, everything becomes a prayer, and you help to save the soul of your loved ones at every moment.

The Gospel is full of miracles that Jesus performed during His lifetime, to help those who came to Him. You might be tempted to think that such miracles no longer exist, and yet God still works wonders today — if we are willing to cooperate. St. Teresa of Ávila said that God has no hands and feet except for yours. You want to work mighty deeds? Discern God's will and do it. You want to preach powerfully? Discern God's will and preach it.

When we pray the Rosary, we are put face-to-face with Jesus and Mary. They make their will known to us. And through prayer, it becomes difficult to face them again until we do God's will. One Hail Mary at a time, our will is put to death. Jesus said, unless a grain of wheat falls to the ground and dies, it remains a grain of wheat, but if it dies, it will bear much fruit. Our will must die, so His will can be done. Mystery by mystery, bead by bead, Mary will lead you down the path of God's will.

4. *Mary is the shortest and best way to Jesus.*

> *God has given us his own mother as our*
> *mother and advocate and has supplied*
> *her with the power to help us.*
>
> — St. Alphonsus Liguori[11]

Mary has an essential role in the life of every Christian. She isn't just a good example. She forms the Body of Christ; she forms you.

If you are one with Christ, if you are a member of His Body, she is your mother. It is the role of Mary to form the Body of Christ. The grace to become a saint, the grace for salvation, and Jesus Christ Himself all come to us from Mary. From Mary,

Christ received His body, His blood, His nourishment, His human formation.

St. Alphonsus teaches that God gives grace according to the mission of the individual, and Mary was given the role of being the Mother of God. The dignity of such a position is beyond our human comprehension. Even before the Incarnation, the angel said to her "Hail, full of grace." She had every grace possible, because through her, Grace would take on human flesh and become man. In fact, at the Incarnation she also carried every grace physically in her womb. Hence, we call her Mediatrix of All Grace. Mary is truly the greatest role model. She is the perfect disciple—no doubt about it—but she is more than just a role model in the life of a Christian. She is our mother. She plays an active and particular role in the life of every Christian. Even in the lives of those who reject her, if they receive any grace, if they have salvation in Jesus Christ, it is only because of Mary's mediation.

Those who excel in the spiritual life, indeed every canonized saint in Heaven, have two great loves: Jesus in the Blessed Sacrament and Mary, their mother. It is in the best interest of every Christian to say yes to Mary, to make an act of acceptance of her as our mother. The greatest of saints totally surrendered their entire lives to Mary without fear of loving her too much. Why? To accept Mary as your mother, to love her, to obey her voice, and to do her will is to make you like Christ. When you accept her and cooperate with her formation, she then takes an active role in your formation. When you spend time with her in prayer, you begin to resemble her just as Christ resembled her. When you spend time with her, you begin to take on her virtues. So much happens when you surrender your life to Jesus through Mary.

Jesus' mission was to provide you with every gift and sacrament necessary for you to be intimately united with Him, and the last thing He did was give you a mother. His very own mother! This motherhood was foretold in Genesis when God the Father warned the serpent, saying, "I will put enmity between you and the woman, and between your offspring and hers" (Gen. 3:15). Now at the Cross, Jesus has made you her offspring in Him. John tells us in Revelation that the dragon goes off to make war against the woman and her offspring. John then says plainly that the offspring of Mary are those who believe in Jesus Christ and cling to the commandments (see Rev. 12:17). You are her offspring, and according to St. Alphonsus Liguori, Mary loves you with all the love of every mother who has ever lived combined. Think of the awe and wonder of a mother looking at her brand-new infant for the first time, how she pays attention to every detail of that child. That is how the Virgin Mary looks at you every single second.

She loves you. But she can't help you unless you cooperate. The Doctor of the Church, St. Bernard of Clairvaux, said,

> In dangers, in doubts, in difficulties, think of Mary, call upon Mary. Let not her name depart from your lips, never suffer it to leave your heart.... With her for guide, you shall never go astray; while invoking her, you shall never lose heart; so long as she is in your mind, you are safe from deception; while she holds your hand, you cannot fall; under her protection you have nothing to fear.
>
> Therefore, call upon her! Don't stop calling upon her.[12]

When the Virgin Mary was present at the Crucifixion of her Son, her love for Him was so intense that the spiritual writers say she felt every agony that Christ felt, but in her soul. Ven. Fulton Sheen says that at the Crucifixion, a single lance was used to pierce two Hearts at the same time. Mary endured the agony of Christ's Crucifixion so as to be able to look at you and say, "My child." It is the will of God the Father that you have a mother that loves you so much. It is the will of God the Father that you have a mother that is so powerful.

In *The Glories of Mary*, St. Alphonsus Liguori says that God is omnipotent by nature, but Mary is omnipotent by grace.[13] At the wedding feast of Cana, it wasn't even Jesus' hour, but at the word of Mary, Jesus was moved. It is the will of God that you have a mother who loves you with the intensity of perfection with which she loves Christ, and a mother who has power even over the Heart of God. You have a mother whose primary concern is turning you into Christ. It is this perfect mother, this powerful mother, this loving mother who has created the Rosary to turn ordinary men into saints, into other Christs.

The Rosary was designed by the Virgin Mary. She looked at the various complications and traps in the world. Then she looked at the needs of her children. She knew the power in the sacraments, the beauty of deep mental prayer. She knew her children needed a way to touch the Heart of God, a process for discerning God's will, fighting spiritual warfare; she took all of this into account and made the perfect prayer, the Holy Rosary.

Be assured of my prayers for you as you embark on this journey. Please pray for me.

> *The prayer of the Rosary, ... after the Holy Liturgy*
> *of the Eucharist, is what most unites us with God*
> *by the richness of the prayers which compose it.*
> *All of them came from heaven, dictated by the*
> *Father, by the Son, and by the Holy Spirit.*
> — Servant of God Lucia dos Santos[14]

CHAPTER 2

The Origins of the Rosary

—Ps. 1:2–4

KNOWING THE ORIGINS AND history of the Rosary is extremely important. The Rosary is one of the most powerful gifts from God to destroy vice, grow in holiness, and wreak havoc on the works of Satan. For this reason, from the moment of its founding, the devil has worked to discourage the praying of the Rosary. By examining how the Rosary was introduced and its organic development in history, we gain key insights that will aid us in practicing this devotion, as well as in sharing it with others. The devil makes use of forces, even within the Church, to discourage the fruitful praying of the Rosary, and yet all the lies of the enemy can be undone and our devotion strengthened by highlighting a few key moments in the Rosary's history.

THE HEART OF THE GOSPEL, THE HEART OF MARY

The Gospels are the origin and the center of the Rosary. The words of the prayers come from the Gospels. The meditations come from the Gospels. It is through the Gospels that we encounter Jesus Christ, and this is the power of the Rosary. There does not exist a more Gospel prayer.

The Rosary also comes straight from the heart of the Blessed Mother. Mary had the Gospels always in her heart; she had the words of the angel Gabriel always in her heart.

There are two necessary elements to the Rosary: the words and the meditations. The words we pray in the Rosary are rooted in Sacred Scripture: the Our Father, given by our Lord to the apostles, and the Hail Mary, uttered by St. Gabriel at the Annunciation and by St. Elizabeth at the Visitation. Therefore, these words come straight from the Heart of God. Jesus Himself spoke the Our Father, Gabriel spoke as a messenger of God the Father, and St. Elizabeth spoke under the inspiration of the Holy Spirit. Meditating on the life of Christ is unlike thinking about any other historical figure, because when you spend time in prayer with Christ, you come into contact with the living God.

Meditating on the life, death, and Resurrection of Christ was widely practiced from the earliest days of the Church. These two main components of the Rosary existed apart at the beginning and in parallel tracks for centuries, but in the heart of Mary they were always one.

The Rosary puts you in the Gospel narrative, where you do not just think about Jesus Christ but rather you meet Him. Even that does not adequately describe what is happening, because in the Rosary, you are looking at Him through the eyes of the one who saw Him most, and you are encountering Him through the heart that loved Him most. In the Rosary, you have the gospel message filtered through the mind and heart of Mary. Remember her goal? To make you like Christ: to form you, to educate you, to grow you into her Son. Remember what happens when you spend time with Mary? You begin to resemble her; she who was most faithful, most virtuous, most pleasing to God.

Both the words and the meditations spring from the very Immaculate Heart of Mary. Think of what we do in the Rosary. We repeat the words of the angel to announce the Incarnation: "Hail Mary, full of grace." From what person do we learn of this event? Was St. Luke there? No. We learn of this from Mary. In the Rosary, at the repetition of the Hail Mary, we take the hand of Mary and walk with her to Jesus Christ in the various stages of His life. Mary's soul magnifies the Lord, and with her prayer, with her protection and intercession, we hear God's voice and see His face more clearly as we pray.

The Hail Mary is indeed directed at Mary, but it is a Christocentric prayer, announcing that the Second Person of the Holy Trinity desires to become man with, in, and through Mary. Scripture tells us that Mary pondered all things in her heart. We might often wonder: What did Mary ponder the most? Was it the wedding at Cana? Was it the institution of the Eucharist? Was it the Crucifixion? Or perhaps the Resurrection?

In the Rosary, we repeat the Hail Mary so many times. Why? Because these words mark the moment the Word became flesh. When Our Lady held the baby Jesus to nurse at her breast, she had to marvel, *God took on flesh and is nursing.* When Jesus hung on the Cross, *God took on flesh and is being put to death like a criminal.* Each and every mystery that we meditate on with Mary began with the Angelic Salutation of St. Gabriel; the Incarnation is at the heart of all she ponders. At the Incarnation she said yes to being the mother of the Savior and the mother of the saved.

The words of the Hail Mary rang out in her heart at every moment as she pondered all things in the depths of her being. The words of the Rosary—Gospel words—and the mysteries of the Rosary—Gospel mysteries—existed in Mary as one, but it took hundreds of years before the meditations of the Gospel and the prayers of the Gospel existed as one in the heart of the Church.

St. Dominic and the First Rosary

I have come to set the earth on fire, and
how I wish it was already blazing!
— Luke 12:49

St. Dominic de Guzmán's life is one of the most significant in all of Christendom. St. Dominic was special even before his conception. His mother, Bl. Jane of Aza, was well known for her compassion for the poor, her piety, and the miraculous effect of her prayers. One evening, she had a prophetic dream. Bl. Jordan of Saxony, head of the Dominican order after St. Dominic's death, gives this account:

> Before Dominic's mother conceived him, she saw in a vision that she would bear in her womb a dog who, with a burning torch in his mouth, seemed to set the whole earth on fire. This was to signify that her child would be an eminent preacher who, by "barking" sacred knowledge, would rouse to vigilance souls drowsy with sin, as well as scatter throughout the world the fire which the Lord Jesus Christ came to cast upon the earth.[15]

At his Baptism, St. Dominic's godmother claimed to have seen a bright star on Dominic's forehead.[16] This star is also how St. Dominic is identified in his iconography.

From a young age, St. Dominic displayed extraordinary virtues and piety. As he grew in wisdom and stature, he dedicated his life to saving souls by prayer, mortification, study, and preaching. As a priest and a Canon Regular of the Cathedral of Osma, St. Dominic was known for his preaching—he was so good that the official name of the religious community he founded, the Dominicans, is the "Order of Preachers." His order adopted a white religious habit similar to that of the Canons Regular.

At the time, the Albigensian heresy was spreading like wildfire and giving rise to several other heretical groups. The Albigensians claimed there are two deities: a good one, who created the spiritual world, and a bad one, who created the material world. They rejected the sacraments and the authority of the Church, ultimately denying the Incarnation of Christ.

Despite his great holiness and extraordinary preaching ability, St. Dominic was not successful at converting the Albigensians. His words were not piercing the hearts of his hearers. Fortunately, he understood well the paradox of Christianity: Unless a grain of wheat falls to the ground and dies, it cannot bear fruit. Conversion and fruitfulness in mission are only possible with divine grace, and divine grace is only obtained through prayer and sacrifice.

St. Dominic offered himself to God as a living sacrifice, and he entered into a time of intense prayer and mortification. His intention was to call down the mercy of God, to have the grace to reach hardened sinners, to unleash the power of the New Testament, to set the world on fire. After several days of prayer and fasting, staying up in vigil night upon night, and mortifying his body, his prayer was finally answered. He suddenly saw in the sky a massive ball of fire coming toward him along with three dazzling angels. The fireball vanished, and he found himself in the presence of the Virgin Mary.

She came to give him a message from Heaven. Here are her most famous words to St. Dominic as noted by Bl. Alan de la Roche, echoed by St. Louis de Montfort, and confirmed by popes:

> At this point Our Lady appeared to him, accompanied by three angels, and she said: "… I want you to know that in this kind of warfare, the battering ram has always been the Angelic Psalter, which is the cornerstone of the New Testament. Therefore, if you want to reach hardened souls and win them over to God, preach my Psalter."[17]

Listen to those words again: "In this kind of warfare, the battering ram …" There is a war going on for our minds and hearts. The war began in the Garden—"I will put enmity between you and the woman, and between your offspring and hers" (Gen. 3:15).

Prior to the coming of Christ, the world was under the dominion of Satan and truly in darkness. How did the light of Christ penetrate this earth? How did Christ break down the walls of the kingdom of Satan? How did hope enter the world? "Hail Mary, full of grace." Those words from the angel Gabriel were the turning point in salvation history.

It is with those words that the veil of darkness was pierced by light. Through those words and Mary's response, the Second Person of the Holy Trinity took on human flesh and became true God and true man. The heart of Mary was already a perpetual yes, but when the offer was made by Gabriel and she formally accepted, it marked the beginning of the end for the kingdom of Satan.

Now think of one of the great promises of Christ: "You are Peter, and on this rock I will build my church, and the gates of Hades will not prevail against it" (Matt. 16:18).

So often in the Church we interpret this to mean that Hell and Satan will not penetrate the Church, that there will always be a small remnant. True, but it also means more than that. Our Lord is magnanimous. The gates of Hell shall not prevail against *you*! The Christian empowered by the Holy Spirit will break down the gates of Hell. No evil will be able to stop you; not even death itself can conquer you. Just as a battering ram must be used repeatedly to penetrate a gate, so we must repeat the Hail Mary with fervor and conviction.

Have the gates of Hell set up around you? Is there a stronghold of lust in your heart? Has the evil one set up walls in your family? How will you break down these gates? With the battering ram, this Angelic Salutation, "Hail Mary, full of grace." Those words always bring light. Those words always bring Christ. At those words, the Father always inclines His ear; at those words the Son always pours out love; at those words the Holy Spirit always responds; at those words the heart of Mary is forever attentive. Hell trembles at these precious words. We can use the battering ram to fight the spiritual battles in our lives; we can repeat the Hail Mary until the gates of Hell come crashing down around us. I have seen it happen in the lives of so many who take this message seriously. Fight. Mary never loses.

Preach my Psalter...

Here is a line that changes history. In it, there is so much to unpack. Mary says, "Preach my Psalter." She doesn't say, "Preach my Rosary." At this time, the Rosary didn't exist, but the Angelic Psalter did, and St. Dominic knew exactly to what she was referring. At that time, it was the habit of consecrated religious to pray the 150 Psalms, which beautifully convey every facet of the human experience. By praying them at particular hours throughout the day, religious would surrender their lives to God.

At this time most people, especially the laity, were illiterate. So, it was a common practice for laypeople to pray their own version of the Psalter. They would carry beads and pray 150 other prayers that were easy to memorize. Some would pray 150 Our Fathers; others would pray 150 Hail Marys. Our Lady was telling St. Dominic to preach the version of the Psalter with 150 Hail Marys. This is very important. "The Rosary" as Our Lady was revealing it wasn't 50 Hail Marys, like we pray today, but 150 Hail Marys. But don't let the number 150 startle you. These Hail Marys are broken up into mysteries and prayed at different points in the day. Mary then went on to instruct St. Dominic to break up the Psalter into groups of ten Hail Marys, which were to be prayed while meditating on different aspects of the life of Christ. St. Louis de Montfort explains:

> Our Lady taught Saint Dominic this excellent method of praying and ordered him to preach it far and wide so as to reawaken the fervor of Christians and to revive in their hearts a love for Our Blessed Lord.... The Rosary said without meditating on the sacred mysteries of our salvation would be almost like a body without a soul.[18]

The importance of combining the Hail Mary with the meditation is also confirmed in an apparition to Bl. Alan, in which Mary said,

> When people say one hundred and fifty Angelic Salutations, this prayer is very helpful to them and is a very pleasing tribute to me. But they will do better still and will please me even more if they say these salutations while meditating on the life, death, and passion of Jesus Christ — for this meditation is the soul of this prayer.[19]

Praying 150 Hail Marys on beads already existed at the time of St. Dominic. What was new was Mary's addition of the meditation on the life of Christ during her Psalter and the specific commissioning of St. Dominic to preach this method of prayer. It is very important to note that at this point only the first half of the Hail Mary as we know it today was prayed. "Hail Mary, full of Grace, the Lord is with thee. Blessed art thou amongst women and blessed is the fruit of thy womb." That is all; the second half was completely absent, and the word "rosary" wasn't used by Our Lady in St. Dominic's commissioning. This is relevant because there are those who would say the way Mary gave the Rosary to St. Dominic is perfect and nothing should be added or removed, and that is not the case.

St. Dominic's obedience to this command to go and preach is also important, because, in addition to the power of the New Testament and the Angelic Salutation, there is also a special grace to do what he is commissioned to do. St. Dominic did as Mary asked, and he was met with evangelical success.

The Second Vatican Council's document *Dei Verbum* states that the study of Sacred Scripture "should be the very soul of sacred theology."[20] We see this lived out in St. Dominic's promotion of the Rosary. The mysteries of the life of Christ preached together with the words of the Incarnation eradicated the false doctrines of the Albigensian heretics. This was established by Bl. Alan and echoed by St. Louis de Montfort's *The Secret of the Rosary*:

> No sooner had Saint Dominic begun preaching the Rosary than hardened sinners were touched and wept bitterly over their grievous sins. Young children performed incredible penances and everywhere that he preached the Holy Rosary such fervor arose that sinners

changed their lives and edified everyone by their penances and change of heart.[21]

This is extremely significant. Here we have a promise from Our Lady to reach hardened sinners and to call down the mercy of God if we promote the Rosary. Jesus and Mary richly blessed St. Dominic by performing many wonders through his hands. He was graced with many apparitions. St. Dominic would prepare for his sermons and missionary preaching by praying the Rosary, and the prophetic dream his mother had came true. St. Dominic was going from place to place setting the world on fire, and God was blessing his ministry. His life was full of wonders, from casting out demons to healing the sick and raising the dead.

The stories from St. Dominic's life are truly incredible, and people who have not experienced such graces might be amazed at them. St. Louis de Montfort acknowledges in his book *The Secret of the Rosary* that the effects of the Rosary are marvelous. What do we make of such stories? This is a reasonable question. First, we look at the character of the individual who is making the claim. Are they honest and good? Then we look at the claim. Is it edifying? Is it in line with the truth of our Faith? If so, then, in charity, it does us no harm to accept it in pious faith.

The apparition of Mary to St. Dominic was later given the title the Apparition of Our Lady of the Rosary. This title is very significant. Mary herself would confirm the power and efficacy of this event at one of the most marvelous Church-approved apparitions in history. If you want to learn more about the life of St. Dominic, I encourage you to read the biography of St. Dominic by Bl. Jordan of Saxony. I highly recommend Bl. Alan de la Roche and St. Louis de Montfort for more in-depth study of this topic.

St. Dominic died on August 6, 1221, but as you will see, his work and influence are far from over.

> *I promise you that if you practice this devotion*
> *and help to spread it, you will learn more from*
> *the Rosary than from any spiritual book. And*
> *what is more, you will have the happiness of being*
> *rewarded by Our Lady in accordance with the*
> *promises that she made to Saint Dominic, Blessed*
> *Alan de la Roche, and to all those who practice*
> *and encourage this devotion that is so dear to her.*
>
> — St. Louis de Montfort[22]

BLESSED ALAN AND THE RENEWAL OF THE PSALTER

Despite St. Dominic's widespread success, after about a century the Marian Psalter fell into obscurity. The ravages and effects of the Black Death played a role in diminishing this devotion; the high death rate hampered the ability to hand on the devotion within certain populations. Priests stopped preaching it, and people stopped praying it. There were small pockets of the faithful that kept the devotion, but it all but dropped from general practice.

Our Lady had her eye on a worldly young man and obtained for him the grace of conversion. Bl. Alan de la Roche was born in 1428, and after his conversion joined the Dominican order. Bl. Alan was widely known and highly respected by all as an illustrious preacher and learned theologian, and he was the one Mary chose to renew devotion to her Rosary, as recounted by St. Louis de Montfort:

One day when he was saying Mass, Our Lord, Who wished to spur him on to preach the Holy Rosary, spoke to him in the Sacred Host:

"How can you crucify Me again so soon?" Jesus said.

"What did you say, Lord?" asked Blessed Alan, horrified.

"You crucified Me once before by your sins," answered Jesus, "and I would willingly be crucified again rather than have My Father offended by the sins you used to commit. You are crucifying Me again now because you have all the learning and understanding that you need to preach My Mother's Rosary, and you are not doing so. If you only did this, you could teach many souls the right path and lead them away from sin—but you are not doing it and so you yourself are guilty of the sins that they commit.[23]

Bl. Alan was also visited by Mary. She made it clear to him that it was she who obtained the grace of his conversion and that this grace of conversion was obtained specifically so that he could be a promoter of the Rosary. St. Dominic himself appeared to Bl. Alan, encouraged him to promote the Rosary, and gave him advice and insights from his own life. "See the wonderful results I have had through preaching the Holy Rosary!" he said. "You and all those who love Our Lady ought to do the same so that, by means of this holy practice of the Rosary, you may draw all people to the real science of the virtues."[24]

Although Bl. Alan had frequent mystical experiences, he was well regarded as a brilliant theologian and an excellent public speaker. He put all these gifts at the service of God to renew devotion to the Rosary and reform the Dominican order. Aside from preaching, Bl. Alan did some writing. His most famous work is *De Dignitate Psalterii.* This is his primary account of the history of the Rosary in the Dominican order, beginning with St. Dominic. His book mixes historical research, sound theology, interesting stories, and many insights from his mystical encounters with Jesus, Mary, and St. Dominic.

Bl. Alan was wildly successful in restoring the Rosary to prominence in the Dominican order and in Catholic culture, so much so that he went out of his way to make it clear that he wasn't the creator of the Rosary and several times emphasized he was only renewing what St. Dominic had received. At the time, there were other forms of the Marian Psalter in circulation, even one that had 150 mysteries for meditation. Bl. Alan again emphasized that his personal mission given to him by God was to restore, revive, and promote the work of his founder, St. Dominic.

The word *rosary* began popping up in some circles when referring to the practice of praying the Marian Psalter. Pious people would say that praying the Ave Maria was like offering Our Lady a rose, and praying the Rosary was like offering her a bouquet or crown of roses. This is obviously a beautiful sentiment and has been proven true in the extraordinary experiences of saintly people, but Bl. Alan was also very particular to keep referring to it as the Marian Psalter so as to make it clear he was referring to the Dominican Rosary, but also because he found it important to keep the connection with the 150 psalms. Although there began to be many stories of holy people seeing roses drop at the feet of Our Lady when the Hail Marys were prayed, Bl. Alan was aware that keeping the word *Psalter* would help to preserve the idea of 150 (fifty Aves, three times per day) instead of simply praying fifty once.

He was critical of people who only prayed fifty Hail Marys and found it very important that the full 150 were prayed; this was a full prayer that would be completed each day. He honored the traditional fifteen mysteries received by St. Dominic, but he emphasized that other mysteries from the life of Christ could be used. In his book, he includes various methods and meditations for praying the Marian Psalter, one of which contains what we now know as the Luminous Mysteries. For Bl. Alan the critical thing was the Hail Marys, with meditation on some aspect of the life of Christ.

Bl. Alan also outlined fifteen promises that Our Lady made to him and to St. Dominic for those who were faithful to praying the Rosary, which we will discuss in detail in a later section. We owe a great deal to Bl. Alan for his work promoting the Rosary and restoring it to its place of prominence in the Church. Because of his efforts, in less than one hundred years the Rosary would take the world stage and remain prominent for the rest of Church history.

St. Pius V and the Prayer of Victory

After the work of Bl. Alan, devotion to the Rosary spread far and became deeply rooted in Catholic life. Bl. Alan died in 1475, and the Rosary had been so thoroughly promoted that St. Teresa of Ávila, born in 1515 in Spain, said that she grew up praying it with her family. The great saints of the Catholic Reformation had a reputation for praying the full Rosary every day. The two great Doctors of the Church, St. Francis de Sales and St. Teresa of Ávila, prayed all the mysteries every day, as did their contemporaries St. Charles Borromeo, St. Thomas of Villanova, St. Ignatius of Loyola, St. Francis Xavier, St. Francis Borgia, and St. Philip Neri, just to name a few. The Rosary was praised by several popes in a row, but the prayer took on new prominence under St. Pius V shortly after the Council of Trent.

This was a turbulent time in Church history. The Church was literally torn in two, and it was under these circumstances that the Rosary began to thrive as the preeminent Christian devotion. The Protestant Reformation began in 1517, and the Church responded by clarifying all her essential teachings at the Council of Trent. The papacy of St. Pius V still impacts the church today. For starters, popes up until this point wore red, but as a Dominican, Pius insisted that he wear his white habit. Every pope since then has also worn white.

As a Dominican from a reformed community, St. Pius V was extremely devoted to the Virgin Mary, and he prayed all the mysteries of the Holy Rosary daily. Of all the popes, St. Pius V had perhaps the greatest impact on Marian devotion. He officially doubled the length of the Hail Mary by adding the second half: "… Jesus. Holy Mary, Mother of God, pray for us sinners now and at the hour of our death." This is extremely significant for a few reasons. Imagine the response today if the pope announced that the Hail Mary was going to be officially changed! This wasn't out of the blue, however; many people were already praying these words, and it was truly for the good of the Church. The second half of the Hail Mary first appeared spontaneously among the people as a result of the Black Death, and it continued to be used in various places and in some religious communities.

The second half of the Hail Mary is actually quite genius. You are praying the prayer to obtain grace now, but also asking for grace at the hour of death at the same time. So if you pray 150 Hail Marys a day for ten years, at the hour of your death, it is as if you had prayed 547,500 all at once. Thanks be to God! The spiritual masters say that along with experiencing the fear of the unknown, the demons assault the dying person with every attack they can muster—but these demonic attacks are like a drop of water in the ocean compared to a single sigh of the Virgin Mary.

This addition was first introduced in the Catechism of the Council of Trent (1566) and later in the official Roman Breviary (1568). One of the arguments some make against the Luminous Mysteries is that a pope shouldn't add to what Our Lady gave to St. Dominic, but here you have the pope not only adding to what was given to St. Dominic but also adding to what was given to us in Sacred Scripture!

In 1569, in the papal bull *Consueverunt Romani Pontifices,* St. Pius V endorsed the Dominican method of praying the Rosary with the Our Father, ten Hail Marys, and fifteen mysteries. He also doubled down on the Rosary coming to us from St. Dominic through the apparition from Our Lady and officially adopted the name *rosary* as the primary description of the Marian Psalter. The Rosary is a combination of vocal prayer and mental prayer with the life of Christ as the subject matter, and St. Pius V recommended the entire Church pray it for protection against sin and heresy, and for the social and temporal welfare of the Church. It is beautiful to see such humility and docility on the part of the Holy Father, recognizing what is fruitful and implementing it for the good of his flock.

These were not at all bureaucratic or political moves. St. Pius V was beloved and renowned for his holiness and devotion, a spiritual giant and a living saint. These changes came only after much prayer, but they were also the result of mystical encounters with Our Lady. St. Pius V was visited by Mary on multiple occasions, and she was the one who commissioned him and inspired him to promote the Rosary.

St. Pius V was known for his love of poverty and austere lifestyle, and he implemented the reforms of the Council of Trent. He standardized the Tridentine Mass as the Mass for the entire Church and declared fellow Dominican, Thomas Aquinas, a Doctor of the

Church. The Church was truly in need of this reform, and St. Pius V, leading by example, restored order and self-control. He battled tirelessly against Protestantism and did everything possible to limit its spread across Europe. Finally, he helped lead the battle against the Islamic Turkish armies who were invading Europe to spread their religion. St. Pius V didn't fight in the battle, but without his leadership all of Europe would have fallen.

In the sixteenth century, the Ottoman Turks reached the pinnacle of their conquests. They had as their final goal the siege of Rome as a sign of Islam's conquest over Christianity. St. Pius V understood clearly what was at stake and the significant advantage the Turks had, never having been defeated in a naval battle up to this point. St. Pius V reached out to every Catholic nation that would join and pleaded with them to come together with his Papal States to form the Holy League, a last stand for Christianity in the West. The Pope understood that they were vastly outnumbered, and if they were going to win, they must have the help of God. His army had to be completely surrendered over to Jesus and Mary — this fight must be won spiritually first, if there was going to be hope for military victory.

St. Pius V ordered all churches to be kept open and that the people of God pray the Rosary as often as possible for victory. Again, in all things St. Pius V requested of his people, he was sure to be a prime example of it first. The pope committed himself to intense fasting, and he spent several hours praying Rosaries. All the soldiers going to battle were also required to pray the Rosary. On the morning of October 7, everyone in the Christian navy attended Mass and received absolution. The banners of their ships were replaced with holy images, and the leader of the Holy League, Don Jon of Austria, wore a relic of the True Cross around his neck, given to him by St. Pius V.

Proving the leadership qualities and faith of St. Pius V in such a perilous circumstance, he placed all his trust in God and Our Lady of the Rosary. As the battle waged on, the Christian force wasn't doing well until the tide was turned with a strong and sudden gust of wind that favored the Christian ships, leaving the Turkish navy decimated after just five hours of battle. The Christians lost 7,500 men, but the Muslims lost around 30,000.

St. Pius V had been discussing temporal matters with his treasurer when all of a sudden, he was overwhelmed with a sense of the presence of God. He paused for a long while looking out at the sky, burst into tears, and declared victory—weeks before the news would officially reach Rome. He credited the victory to Our Lady and the petitioning of the Rosary, stating that October 7 would be the feast of Our Lady of Victory.

When we totally surrender ourselves over to Jesus and Mary, especially when we do so on their terms—when we go all in—Mary never loses. So many hopeless battles have been won by the Mother of God for those who have placed their hope in her and the power of the Rosary. The Battle of Lepanto is just one example of the power of the Rosary to impact temporal affairs. Confidence in the Rosary and its power was on full display for all Christendom and for all of history.

Two years after the death of St. Pius V, Pope Gregory XIII changed the feast day from Our Lady of Victory to Our Lady of the Rosary. Keep in mind this reference to Our Lady of the Rosary, the same title given to the original apparition of Mary to St. Dominic. This connection between the Rosary and victory is so important—they go hand in hand. Never was it known that Mary left anyone unaided.

*By the rosary the darkness of heresy has
been dispelled, and the light of the Catholic
faith shines out in all its brilliancy.*

—Pope St. Pius V[25]

St. Louis de Montfort: A Marian Prophet

I first started praying the Rosary when I was in college. I was battling the vice of lust at the time and found that when I prayed the Rosary and frequented the sacraments, I stood a chance against my demons. When I prayed multiple Rosaries, I might have moments of struggle, but I would persevere.

My only exposure to the Rosary at that point had been a pamphlet that I got from campus ministry and a little white and blue booklet called *Our Lady of Fatima's Peace Plan from Heaven.* So naturally, I wanted to learn more about the Rosary, since I was relying on praying it so often. When I went to the local Catholic bookstore, I came across a priceless gem of spiritual literature, *The Secret of the Rosary* by St. Louis de Montfort.

St. Louis de Montfort was one of the most influential Marian spiritual writers of the twentieth century, although he was born in the seventeenth century. His writings were rediscovered in the twentieth century, so he is quite literally a prophet for our times. St. Louis de Montfort's books have impacted so many holy people in the "modern" Church. St. John Paul II said that reading St. Louis de Montfort's books was a turning point in his life, so much so that he took a line from *True Devotion to Mary* and made it his papal motto, "*Totus Tuus*" (totally yours).

St. Louis de Montfort stands as a flaming torch in the night, guiding the way to the Heart of Jesus with, in, and through Mary. His name is practically synonymous with Marian consecration. This is partially because, although all the saints practiced intense

Marian devotion and lived a life consecrated to Jesus through Mary, there were actually very few books on the topic of the Rosary and Marian consecration that were short, intense, and didn't compromise. I believe that this was the plan of the Immaculata, and I strongly encourage you to read his writings too. They are short, full of zeal and confidence.

I came across *The Secret of the Rosary* at a time in my life when I wanted answers. Why was it so hard to be good? I knew I was called to be holy, but I didn't have a clear plan on how to do that. I didn't find the answers I needed in my church; at that time, the attitude seemed to be, "If it feels good, do it." I was very conflicted. Fasting didn't feel good, but many saints were telling me to do it. Praying multiple Rosaries was working, but some friends were acting like that was extreme.

Right off the bat, St. Louis de Montfort answered my first question: Is praying more than one Rosary extreme? In his opening letter to sinners, he says: "We should eagerly crown ourselves with these roses from Heaven, and recite the entire Rosary every day, that is to say three Rosaries each of five decades."[26]

In his section to children, he says: "Of course it would be too much to expect you to say the whole fifteen mysteries every day, but do say at least five mysteries."[27] I have known children who have prayed all the mysteries every day, not to mention the children of Fatima, but it is clear that balance and discernment are key.

De Montfort hammers home the idea that the Rosary isn't simply a pious devotion; it is actually theological genius, managing to integrate all of the essential forms of prayer and the Gospels. A more brilliant prayer doesn't exist. He doesn't shy away from comparing the Rosary to other prayers, such as the Psalms of David, and gives several examples from the lives of the saints. He details the divine origins of the Rosary as it was handed down to St. Dominic, backing everything up with historical nuggets of wisdom. "It would hardly be possible for me to put into words how much Our Lady thinks of the Holy Rosary and of how she vastly prefers it to all other devotions," he asserts. "Neither can I sufficiently express how highly she rewards those who work to preach the devotion, to establish it and spread it, nor on the other hand how firmly she punishes those who work against it."[28]

St. Louis de Montfort is adamant that the Rosary is so excellent a prayer for conforming us to Christ that the enemy of our souls will do everything possible to get us to stop praying it. The devil will use ignorant people, he will use "intellectual" people, and he will use every possible means to convince us to abandon this holy practice. Some work against the Rosary and don't even realize it. St. Louis de Montfort says to resist these temptations:

> This is one of the devil's traps; heretics of the past who denied Tradition have fallen into it and over-critical people of today are falling into it too without even realizing it.
>
> People of this kind refuse to believe what they do not understand or what is not to their liking, simply because of their own spirit of pride and independence.[29]
>
> Finally, my dear Brother, the Daily Rosary has so many enemies that I look upon the grace of persevering in it until death as one of the greatest favors Almighty God can give us.[30]

I have read his book on the Rosary perhaps more times than I have read any other book. That raises the obvious question: If his book is so great, why am I writing this book—and why are you reading it?

His book was written for an audience of the 1700s. A lot has happened since then, in the Church and in the world. The culture has changed, and thus the tactics of the devil to get us to abandon the Rosary have changed. The addictions we face and the availability of vice are unlike anything St. Louis de Montfort could have imagined. He couldn't possibly address all the circumstances that we face today.

There have been good changes in the world too. We have had major Marian apparitions and the influence of great saints such as St. John Bosco, Mother Teresa, St. Josemaría Escrivá, and the Fatima children. And what about the Luminous Mysteries? Where do those fit into the 150 framework? In de Montfort's day, most women didn't work outside the home. What role does the Rosary play in the life of a working mom with several kids and a husband who isn't a practicing Catholic? How do you integrate the Rosary into modern family life? These, and many more, are legitimate questions.

St. Louis de Montfort held up the Rosary as the answer to the problems of the modern world at a time in the Church when it seemed like nobody had a good answer. Today, we pick up where St. Louis de Montfort left off.

Our Lady of Lourdes: Mary Promotes the Rosary Herself

On February 11, 1858, Bernadette Soubirous wandered into the Grotto of Massabielle as she waited for her sister and a friend to gather firewood. Suddenly Bernadette saw a beautiful woman:

> Raising my eyes again, I saw Her smiling at me most graciously and seeming to invite me to come nearer. But I was still afraid.... Then I thought of saying my prayers.

> I put my hand in my pocket. I took out the rosary I usu-
> ally carry on me.... While I was saying my rosary, I was
> watching as hard as I could. She was wearing a white
> dress reaching down to her feet, of which only the toes
> appeared. The dress was gathered very tight at the neck
> by a hem from which hung a white cord. A white veil
> covered her head and came down over her shoulders and
> arms almost to the bottom of her dress. On each foot I
> saw a yellow rose. The sash of the dress was blue, and
> hung down below her knees. The chain of the rosary was
> yellow; the beads white, big, and widely spaced.[31]

Notice. Bernadette had the habit of carrying her rosary, and her first instinct was to reach for it. The Virgin Mary would keep track of the prayers on her own set of beads, and when the Rosary was over, the Virgin Mary disappeared.

Our Lady appeared eighteen times to St. Bernadette. Each time, the young St. Bernadette would go down to the grotto and begin the Rosary, and then Our Lady would appear. The apparition would usually last the length of a Rosary. Mary always had the rosary with her, and by the end of the apparitions, thousands would be gathered at the grotto to pray the Rosary with St. Bernadette, although St. Bernadette would be the only one to see her.

This is important for us to note: *Not one of the other thousands who eventually gathered at the grotto were able to see Mary, but she was present.* So too, when we pray the Rosary, we should have confidence that she is present. As you touch your beads, have confidence that, just as she did with St. Bernadette, she is keeping track of each bead and receiving your prayer. Trust her!

There are two things to keep in mind. First, the sign. When an authentic apparition of Mary occurs and she asks for something—in this case, she asks for a chapel to be built—she knows that authorities need a sign. We simply can't believe every person that claims that Mary wants something. And when a sign is needed, Our Lady provides the sign, and it is deeply meaningful. Think of Our Lady of Guadalupe. The bishop wanted a sign of roses, but what he got was not just roses. People barely even remember the roses because he got a *tilma* that defied science and has so much meaning even to this day.

At Lourdes the sign was deeply meaningful as well. Our Lady of Lourdes told St. Bernadette to eat of the vegetation and to wash herself in the spring. Bernadette hesitated because this seemed ridiculous. There was no vegetation, only some shrubs, and there was no spring, only dirt. But afterward, to the shock and amazement of all, water flowed from that very spot—water that had healing properties, deliverance properties.

Our Lady knew that people would flock to this spot, so she chose a perfect place. Practically, the grotto is simply beautiful. People get into the baths of this miraculous water, pouring their hearts out to Our Lady as a reminder of Baptism. And if you have ever been to Lourdes, you know the grotto is a Rosary sanctuary. Each night they have a Rosary procession in Rosary Square, and there are countless shops that are lined with images of Our Lady of Lourdes, images of Mary that have the rosary around her right arm. There, she became a living image of Rosary promotion.

For me, Lourdes is one of the most wonderful places on earth. When a person goes down into the grotto, they are often overcome with emotion and a sense of the presence of Mary. At Lourdes every day is a Marian feast day. On average five million people a year travel to Lourdes from all over the world, and those five million people—whatever their reason for going—encounter Mary's Rosary apostolate. Our Lady herself promotes the Rosary to the millions who visit in person, but also to all those across the world who learn about the apparition.

There is one more important element about Our Lady of Lourdes: Her name isn't Our Lady of Lourdes. Again, remember, with Mary everything is significant. When Bernadette asked her name on March 25, the feast of the Annunciation, the Virgin Mary responded with the following words: "I am the Immaculate Conception." This response sent shock waves throughout the Church, similar to the shock waves when Jesus said "I Am" when He was being arrested in the Garden.

"I am the Immaculate Conception." What could this mean? How can she be a conception? Theologians racked their brains. Our Lady said a single sentence which would take many books to explain, but essentially, when the theology is parsed out, she is the Spouse of the Uncreated Immaculate Conception, the Holy Spirit. She is so perfectly united to the will of God that she is the created Immaculate Conception, and as true spouse she takes His name. This was further developed in the theology of St. Maximilian Kolbe.

Why would Mary reveal such a thing? One, because it's true, but also to astound the theologians. Such a profound message, a deep theological truth, was revealed by a humble little girl with a rosary, Bernadette Soubirous. The Rosary is for the intellectual giants and the poor peasants.

Our Lady of Lourdes, pray for us.

> *In her apparition at Lourdes, in 1858, the Mother*
> *of God held in her arms the rosary, and through*
> *St. Bernadette, recommended to us the recital*
> *of the Rosary. We can conclude, therefore, that*
> *the prayer of the Rosary makes the Immaculate*

*happy. Moreover, with this prayer we can easily
obtain great graces and divine blessings.*

— St. Maximilian Kolbe[32]

OUR LADY OF FATIMA: "PRAY THE ROSARY EVERY DAY"

The apparition of Our Lady of Fatima is the most investigated Catholic event in Church history, with the most witnesses and highest level of approval. The site has been visited multiple times by different popes and has a feast on the universal calendar. Two of the three seers, Sts. Francisco and Jacinta, were canonized as saints in 2017; St. Jacinta's body, exhumed fifteen years after her death, was found to be incorrupt.

The "miracle of the sun," the sign provided by Mary, was witnessed by over seventy thousand people of all backgrounds, and no other Marian apparition has been so thoroughly reviewed by the Vatican, especially because part of its message predicted an assassination attempt on a pope, which was eventually carried out against Pope St. John Paul II on the liturgical feast of Our Lady of Fatima, May 13, 1981.

In order to understand the massive significance of Fatima, particularly in light of the history of the Rosary, it is important to reflect on its historical context. Our Lady in 1917 was making a preemptive strike to prepare the Church for the conflicts of the modern world. The twentieth century saw the rise of secularism and militant atheism. Relativism was dominating the culture, and aspects of modernism had even found their way into the Church. There were also more religious martyrdoms in the twentieth century than in all the previous centuries combined. Humanity would see the rise of fascist and communist regimes, two world wars, genocides, and massive political turmoil. And so, at Fatima

Mary also had to prepare us for the sexual and technological revolutions yet to come.

Pope Pius X put out an encyclical on September 8, 1907, the feast of the Nativity of Mary, warning of the dangers of modernism: Namely, the attempt to change the Church by downplaying the divine, thus making the Church more of a social institution rather than a divine one. The seeds were planted to diminish the sacrifice of Christ on the Cross and His Real Presence in the Eucharist. This is just a glimpse of the landscape that Mary was witnessing when she decided to intervene by appearing in the humblest location to the humblest of people.

On May 13, 1917, Our Lady appeared to three poor, uneducated shepherd children. Jacinta, the youngest seer, was only seven years old. Her brother Francisco was eight, and Lucia, her cousin, was ten. The little peculiarities associated with the children's accounts speak to the authenticity of their experience. For example, Francisco couldn't hear Our Lady, he could only see her—unlike the two girls, who could both see and hear her. The message of Our Lady to the children at that time must also give us pause today: When Lucia asked Mary if Francisco would go to Heaven, Mary said that he would, but he would first have to pray many Rosaries. This eight-year-old boy only lived to be ten, and was a relatively good child—probably rambunctious and rebellious, but living in a much simpler time. How pure must Heaven be, that he had to pray many Rosaries before he could go there?

The effect of the vision on the children also speaks to the veracity of what happened there. Francisco was radically transformed into a model of virtue and piety, making it his goal to console the hidden Jesus in the tabernacle.

Our Lady appeared six times, and at every apparition, her message was essentially the same: "Pray the rosary every day in honor of Our Lady of the Rosary, to obtain peace for the world . . . because only she can help you."[33]

Remember, Mary was here instructing young children — there is no "age limit" when it comes to praying the Rosary. It is a powerful tool of intercession for every believer, of every age. Whether we like it or not and whether we obey or not, Mary is asking even little children to commit to at least a daily Rosary.

The consequences of sin were made clear in the third apparition; the Virgin Mary opened her hands, the earth opened up, and the children were given a vision of Hell. Not just a word or instruction about avoiding Hell, the Mother of God literally gave them a vision of Hell. Then she said, "You have seen hell, where the souls of poor sinners go. To save them, God wishes to establish in the world devotion to My Immaculate Heart. If what I say to you is done, many souls will be saved and there will be peace."[34]

Why is she doing this? What is she teaching us? Again, think of the climate we live in. Many of us have heard with our own ears that everybody goes to Heaven. Even in Catholic education the topic of Hell is tiptoed around. I experienced it myself, and I was teaching eighth grade, far past the age of reason!

Now, I am not advocating for scare tactics; however, Hell is not a place you end up by accident. It is a choice that people make knowingly and willingly.

Knowing that false teachings against Hell were entering the Church, Mary chose to give the most intense catechesis in the form of this horrific vision. In so doing, she bestowed on us an act of mercy: clear catechesis with sound teaching on morality. This is a message of hope and not one of fear. Mary is telling us that God wishes to save people through her Immaculate Heart.

Pray the Rosary because it brings peace. Pray the Rosary because it saves souls, including our own.

And then Our Lady requested an addition to the Rosary: "When you pray the Rosary, say after each mystery: O my Jesus, forgive us our sins, save us from the fire of hell. Lead all souls to heaven, especially those who are most in need of your mercy." The Blessed Virgin's preeminent concern is for the salvation of souls, and her message has a clear urgency. At every decade of the Rosary, she is asking that we make direct appeal to Jesus (through Mary) to save souls; it bears fruit even in those who are farthest away from God.

In addition to this, let me mention an important Latin axiom concerning prayer: *Lex orandi, lex credendi, lex vivendi.* The law of prayer, is the law of belief, is the law of living. In short, how we pray impacts what we believe and that impacts how we live. Praying to Jesus for the forgiveness of our sins to avoid the fires of Hell establishes in us a deeper belief of the eternal consequences of sin, which will change how we live. The adding of this prayer does obtain the grace we request, but it is also catechetical. In an age of moral relativism, where many want mercy without repentance, Our Lady keeps salvation before our eyes as the most important intention in every mystery. In the apparition, Our Lady says something similar: "Pray, pray very much, and make sacrifices for sinners; for many souls go to hell, because there are none to sacrifice themselves and to pray for them."[35]

She is inviting the children to pray and do penance. She is inviting us to pray and do penance. We have a role to play in the salvation of others. She is preaching this for several reasons, but primarily because it works. Prayer and penance work! Do you have a family member who is on the highway to Hell? You can help save them!

Our Lady came to Fatima not to scare children and punish us by asking everyone to pray the Rosary. She came to save us. She came to set the captives free. She came to give us the key to remove the shackles and bondage of sin and addiction. Don't view the daily Rosary as a burden but as a source of freedom.

I mentioned that the devil hates the Rosary because it truly is his undoing and the prayer that helps us to encounter Christ most. The devil has used unbelievers and skeptics to try to discourage the praying of the Rosary, at times by saying it is pious and not for learned people or by saying it wasn't given to St. Dominic. At Fatima Our Lady put the matter to rest.

Although we can't cover the entire apparition here, we will take a close look at her last action of the last apparition. Everything is significant; Mary is intentional. Authentic Marian apparitions have depth, weight, and detail. What she wears is significant, and what she does is significant. Her name is extremely significant, and she even says as much. In previous appearances, she told the children: "You must come here every month, and in October I will tell you who I am."

On October 13, 1917, she tells the children to continue to say the Rosary every day, and then she says to the three children her name: "I am the Lady of the Rosary."[36] She is wearing all white, and on her white garment she has a single symbol, a star. The children saw various apparitions in the sky, but what did the skeptics and atheists see when they tried to catch a glimpse of her for themselves? A dancing sun, a fireball in the sky, coming toward the earth.

Think about that for a moment. What was the name of the apparition to St. Dominic in the thirteenth century? Our Lady of the Rosary. What did St. Dominic wear during his apparition? All white. What was the symbol that represented St. Dominic in his iconography? A star. At the apparition of Our Lady of the Rosary, what did St. Dominic see? A fireball in the sky coming toward the earth.

At Fatima, Mary herself requested we pray the Rosary every day. The children of Fatima, by the time they died, were so transformed by the presence of Mary and by their visions that they prayed many Rosaries a day. Francisco prayed the Rosary virtually nonstop.

Some people will say, "Well, you don't have to believe it." And it's true—you don't. But authorities at the highest levels of the Church have said this is of supernatural origin. This happened. Our Lady appeared at Fatima for you. Will you ignore her? I hope not.

That being said, we need to be very careful in how we encourage others to pray the Rosary, especially new Catholics. We should never guilt or shame somebody into praying the Rosary through fear of Hell or damnation. Our goal should be to inspire, promote, and educate. "We must consider how to rouse one another to love and good works" (Heb. 10:24). We can focus on the encouragement of Sr. Lucia, the oldest and longest-living Fatima visionary.

> The Most Holy Virgin in these last times in which we live has given a new efficacy to the recitation of the Rosary to such an extent that there is no problem, no matter how difficult it is, whether temporal or above all spiritual, in the personal life of each one of us, of our families … that cannot be solved by the Rosary. There is no problem, I tell you, no matter how difficult it is, that we cannot resolve by the prayer of the Holy Rosary.[37]

St. John Paul II: Totus Tuus

On multiple occasions I have accidentally caught myself referring to St. John Paul II as "my dear friend." It just comes out and catches me off guard, and I am quick to clarify that I never actually met him, yet I do genuinely consider him a friend because St. John Paul

II was extremely influential in my early formation. I feel that I have a deep understanding of his heart, due in no small way to the fact that he poured himself out so openly for young people.

Like St. Dominic, Karol Wojtyla's mother had a prophetic vision of her son. According to George Weigel, she proclaimed: "My Lolek will be a great man someday."[38] (Lolek was the diminutive form of Karol.) Their family, like most Polish families, had a great love for the Virgin Mary. Karol's mother died just before his ninth birthday, and upon learning of his mother's death, this heartbroken boy ran to the parish church and dropped to his knees before an image of Mary. The young Karol said to the Mother of Christ, "You must be my mother now."

Let that sink in. Think of this from the perspective of Mary. A boy who just lost his mother makes a heartfelt consecration. If you know Mary, you know she was deeply moved by this and that she takes this kind of entrustment very seriously. Karol Wojtyla accepted her, and she accepted him.

As a boy, Karol might not have heard of Our Lady of Fatima, but he saw the fruits of what she was warning about. He saw first-hand Russia spreading her errors. Karol lived in Poland during the height of the Nazi invasion and later under the shadow of Russian occupation. He had an extremely difficult life, and indeed, all of Poland was suffering.

Karol said that one of the most influential witnesses in his life was that of his father, who not only took Karol's catechesis and formation seriously but also led by example. On more than one occasion, young Karol would wake up in the middle of the night and catch his father on his knees praying the Rosary. Sometimes he would wake up very early and find the same thing. This sort of witness leaves on young souls a profound and lasting impact that can never be erased.

I didn't have a father growing up, and when I first heard this and the impact that it had on Karol, I thought to myself, "I want to be a man like that." The world would be different if all fathers lived like this. The greatest inheritance Karol's father gave him was a love for Mary and the Rosary. This love for the Rosary was deeply ingrained upon his heart, was part of his culture, and was the strength of his family. Karol said that his home was his first seminary.

As a young man Karol was deeply impacted by a mystic and playwright who acted as a spiritual director. Jan Tyranowski would introduce Karol to the writings and spirituality of St. John of the Cross and St. Teresa of Ávila. Karol became a young man of deep contemplative prayer, so much so that he attempted to join the Carmelites, but his bishop saw another path. This is critically important for understanding the young man's love and appreciation for the Rosary, which can only be properly utilized if you understand it in its deepest contemplative dimension. Karol understood this: The Rosary isn't just repeating the Hail Mary; it is first and foremost an encounter with Christ in the mysteries. The Hail Marys act as sort of a background song that stirs up the spirit, keeps distractions at bay, and acts as a timer for the encounter.

As pope, St. John Paul II took as his papal motto *Totus Tuus.* Many are familiar with the motto, but what most people haven't reflected on is that it wasn't just a motto for himself. By taking on this motto, he was proclaiming the Marian lifestyle as one suitable for the universal Church and as the spirituality for every person.

He was giving testimony of the power of Marian consecration in his own life, but that does what a good testimony is meant to do — spark interest in others, which is why we have seen a boom in total consecration. St. John Paul II put a spotlight on St. Louis de Montfort, Mariology, and total consecration unlike any other individual in human history.

Also, it isn't just a motto; it isn't just a testimony. It is a prayer. He totally gave his pontificate to Mary, and do you know what Mary does when you give her everything? She accepts it, and she transforms it, and she gives you everything. Mary is not outdone in generosity. What you give to her, she transforms and offers back to you manifold. What do you want of me, Mary? That is what St. John Paul II was saying. And as we will see, Mary wanted a radical change: not a removal of the Rosary but an increase.

St. John Paul II was Polish. The history of Poland is the history of a nation that consecrated herself fully to Mary—even at the highest levels of government—and of a people who were repeatedly invaded and attacked, yet found refuge under the mantle of Mary. For the Polish people, yes, Mary is a loving mother; yes, Mary is a good queen. But she is also a fierce warrior. There are so many stories of Mary defending the Polish people in battle. Ponder for a moment the image of the Black Madonna of Czestochowa. She wears a scar on her face. The history of Our Lady of Czestochowa is one of battle. St. John Paul II helped to overthrow the communist regimes—the work of Satan as warned by Our Lady of Fatima—not by physical arms, but by spiritual ones.

On May 13, 1981, the feast of Our Lady of Fatima, St. John Paul II was shot in St. Peter's Square. The details of his survival are nothing short of miraculous. When questioned about the event, St. John Paul II said, "One finger was pulling the trigger, but another finger was guiding the bullets." Only an atheist could deny the connection with the message of Fatima. St. John Paul II himself went to Fatima many times to pay homage to Our Lady of the Rosary, and he had the bullet that pierced his body placed in her crown. His pontificate and the message of Our Lady of the Rosary at Fatima are one.

All of this is to give you some context behind one of the boldest moves in Rosary history. St. John Paul II loved Mary. St. John Paul II was a mystic, and he could see the evils spreading around the world and in the Church. He loved the Rosary, prayed all the mysteries at least once every day, was often seen with a rosary in hand, and was well known for giving out rosaries to all who visited him.

As he put it, "The Rosary is my favorite prayer."[39]

St. John Paul II understood the Rosary. He knew that it was more than just a succession of Hail Marys, that in the Rosary you have a catechesis on the life of Christ and an encounter with the Son of God. In the story of Christ's life, we have a recapitulation of what the human experience is meant to be, and up until St. John Paul II's pontificate, the Rosary had a major gap in the recounting of that story. A grace remembered is a grace renewed, and St. John Paul II could see in the world the crises of baptized unbelievers, attack on the sanctity of marriage, attack on Marian devotion, the effects of weak preaching, the denial of the divinity of Christ, a downplaying of the sacred priesthood, and a loss of faith in the Real Presence. Just as St. Dominic responded in a particular way to the Albigensian heresy that challenged the faithful of his time, St. John Paul II understood that what is needed to become a saint today is a renewal of grace in these areas by a renewal of attention to these aspects of the life of Christ. We needed more contemplation on the gospel message, so in *Rosarium Virginis Mariae* he added the Luminous Mysteries: "For the Rosary to become more fully a 'compendium of the Gospel,' it is fitting to add … a meditation on certain particularly significant moments in his public ministry."[40]

I accept the Luminous Mysteries on faith, but they also make sense to me. The three sets of mysteries were always very good, and like a stool with three legs, they were sufficient — any less and you wouldn't grasp the essential story of Christ. But the entire public ministry of Christ was missing. Look at the chair you are sitting on or the dinner table that your family gathers around to eat. How many legs does it have? Why four legs and not three or five? Four legs on a table are better because they provide the most stability and evenly distribute weight, making a firm, balanced, and complete foundation. So, too, including the public ministry of Christ provides a solid foundation.

This change takes nothing away from the original mysteries; nothing is lost. He added more Christ to the Rosary, not less. He knew that this would be a disrupter; in fact, he anticipated it. Personally, I love the Luminous Mysteries, and I know my eucharistic faith especially has been profoundly impacted by the daily praying of these mysteries.

> *It would be impossible to name all the*
> *many Saints who discovered in the Rosary*
> *a genuine path to growth in holiness.*
> — St. John Paul II[41]

The Rosary: Today and Forever

> *Modern times are dominated by Satan and will*
> *be more so in the future. The conflict with hell*
> *cannot be engaged by men, even the most clever.*
> *The Immaculata alone has from God the promise*
> *of victory over Satan. However, assumed into*
> *Heaven, the Mother of God now requires our*
> *cooperation. She seeks souls who will consecrate*
> *themselves entirely to her, who will become in her*

*hands effective instruments for the defeat of Satan
and the spreading of God's kingdom upon earth.*
— St. Maximilian Kolbe[42]

I have been blessed to have had very clear moments of being called to pray the Rosary and very clear moments of being called to promote the Rosary. When I knew it was the will of God for me to pray the entire Rosary every day, I was forced to answer the question: What does it mean to pray the Rosary today and every day?

The thirteenth century, the sixteenth century, the eighteenth century, even the beginning of the twentieth century doesn't hold a candle to the perversion and wickedness of this present age. Remember when Our Lady gave the children a vision of Hell and how souls were falling into Hell like snowflakes—that was 1917.

The world is very different now. Consider that the average person looks at a screen—either television, smartphone, or tablet—somewhere between eight to twelve hours per day. We are all bombarded with nonstop propaganda. A young person can see ads, listen to music, play games, and watch movies that all exist in a worldview where God doesn't exist. Many good Catholic parents have come to me in dismay that their children have all fallen away from the Faith. How could this happen? There are a lot of factors, but no doubt the negative influence of the world has outweighed their influence. So much content that we are exposed to every day is run by algorithms designed to keep our attention captive; just as some bait or lures are meant to overpower the natural instincts of the prey, certain algorithms and programs are designed to weaken us to keep our attention and gain influence. So many people are truly slaves to devices. We would rather look at our screens than our own family members.

These same algorithms are being used by pornography companies. In a recent study, as many as 91.5 percent of men and 60.2 percent of women reported consuming pornography in the last month.[43] Children are exposed to pornography as early as nine years old. Imagine telling St. Dominic or Pope Pius V that there is a brothel in every child's pocket and that in many cases the children are then groomed to create pornography themselves. They couldn't fathom it. Of course, the device is just a tool; it is from our hearts that corruption comes, but it is so much easier to be led astray with modern technology at our fingertips. This is just one aspect of our culture, not to mention drugs, alcohol, gambling; the list can go on and on. We live in a post-Christian era. People quickly question the meaning of life, and some want out and want God, but while people are trying to escape, many can't, because of the addictive nature of their vices (and devices). They are looking for meaning and freedom, but they are stuck in slavery to sin.

There is freedom. I have found freedom from these things; Mary has given me strength to fight under her standard. She extends her hand to you, and I extend my hand to you as well, to join in the battle. Take up your weapon. Take up the Rosary to be your means of transformation and liberation. Perhaps you are one of the few not enslaved by sin, but you know other people who are. Mary is looking for people to make reparation by praying more and offering it as their victimhood for the salvation of others. You might have family members who are lost. Our Lady will help you to rescue them.

When I received the tugging on my heart and the conviction from God that I had to promote the Rosary, I seriously asked the question: Do I promote one, two, three, four? I knew interiorly that four, as difficult as it was, is the correct answer. I was afraid, however, because in the eyes of the world that would seem extreme. So I looked to the saints. What did they promote? They promoted the full Rosary as they knew it, and then worked backward to accommodate each person's circumstances and each person's need. So that is what I will be doing. Examine the benefits of the full Rosary, and then pray to determine what is right for you.

As one who was lost in sin, I know that a special grace is given after the fourth Rosary, and I know that if you persevere in all four, not only will you overcome your vices but every aspect of your spiritual life will be elevated. With this as my experience, how can I not promote four? This is the state of the Rosary today. There is a growing movement of people from every age group, walk of life, and demographic who have already accepted the entire Rosary as their path to sanctity. More and more are praying the entire Rosary every day, as a way of life. This lifestyle requires tips and advice and balance, which I hope to provide you if you are interested in going all in. St. John Paul II noted that countless saints found in the Rosary a sure path to holiness, and it is fitting that the saints of our generation, the most wicked generation, should be even more devoted to Jesus through Mary and the Rosary.

These people who have persevered in the Rosary as a foundation for their spiritual lives have become apostles in their local communities. The last chapter of this book will be a series of short testimonies from ordinary people I personally know whose lives have been changed by the power of the Rosary. It is my hope that by the end of this book, you too might feel the call to be an apostle of the Rosary.

The Blessed Virgin Mary repeated several times
what she had told me on other occasions — that
I was to be the "Dominic of these times in
spreading devotion to the Rosary."

— St. Anthony Mary Claret[44]

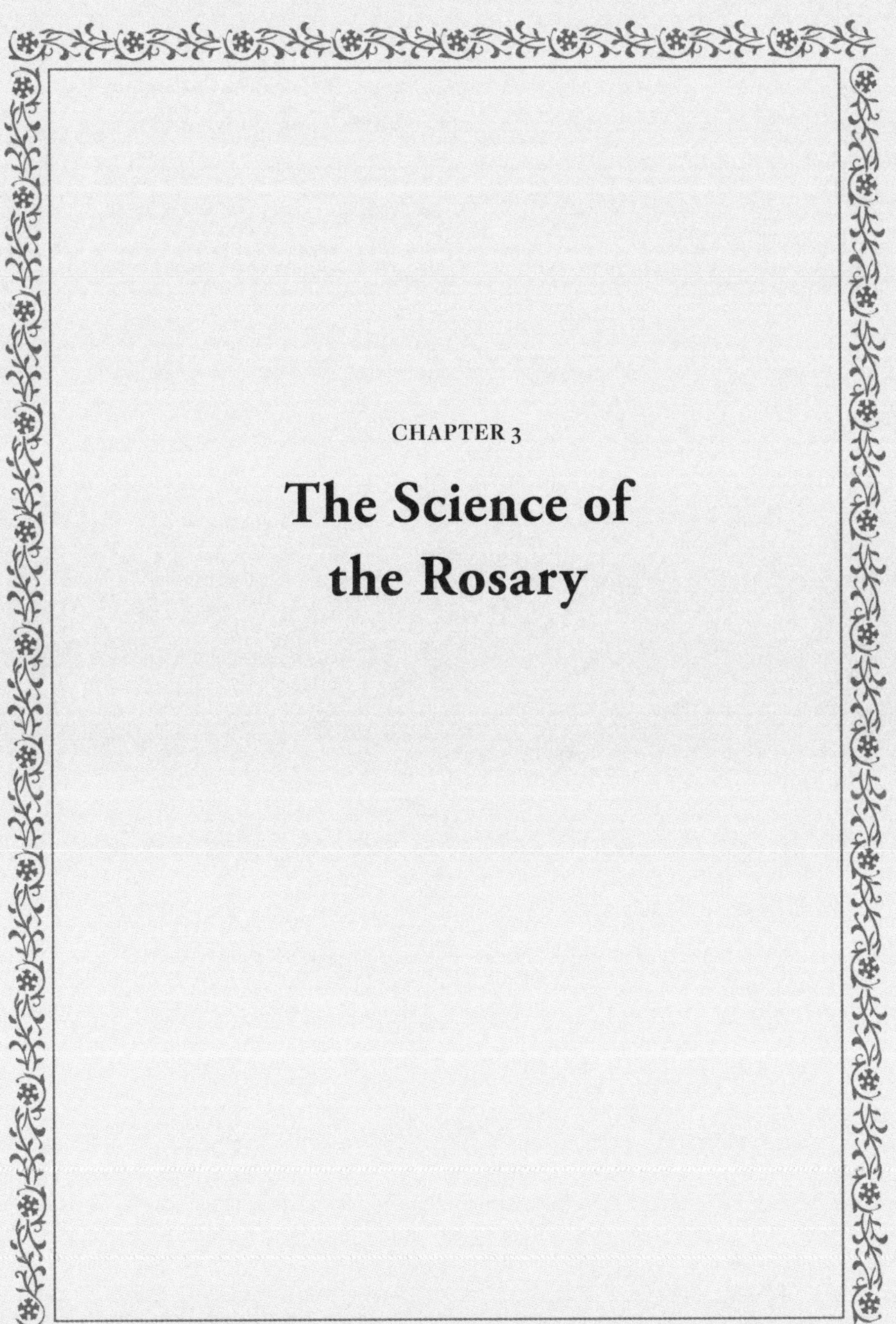

CHAPTER 3

The Science of the Rosary

*There is no surer means of calling down God's blessing
upon the family ... than the recitation of the Rosary.*
— Pope Pius XII[45]

*The Rosary is the glory of the Roman Church. It
takes its place after the Mass and the Sacraments.*
— Pope St. John XXIII[46]

*The prayer of the Rosary is perfect, because of
the praises it offers, the lessons it teaches, the
graces it obtains, and the victories it achieves.*
— Pope Benedict XV[47]

I N THIS CHAPTER, WE will examine why the Rosary is so powerful. The Rosary is more of a divine science than a pious devotion, a prayer for the simple and for the scholar. The Rosary is for everybody. Anybody can pray it, but there is one prerequisite: humility.

HUMILITY: THE ONE THING YOU MUST BRING

God resists the proud, but gives grace to the humble.
— *James 4:6, NABRE*

Humility is essential for praying the Rosary. Without humility, you won't even pick up the beads. You must bring to Mary your weakness and insecurity, coming to her with empty hands. What is humility? "Humility is truth," according to St. Teresa of Ávila.[48] It is twofold: The truth about yourself and the truth about God.

Jesus called the devil a liar from the beginning; pride and lies go together. When the devil tempts us, he uses lies and partial truths to lead us to sin.

So, what is the truth about us? The truth is that humans are weak physically, even the strongest of us. We get sick. We die. Our weak physical condition, when seen clearly, puts everything into perspective. Suffering endears men to Christ. When we physically suffer, we aren't so worried about the kind of car we drive or our status in the world; we see clearly. This is one reason I especially encourage people to promote the Rosary to family and friends who are suffering. Suffering disposes the soul to cry out to God.

Humans are also weak morally. This truth is essential for true humility. We are all inclined to sin. We all suffer from a threefold concupiscence. We lie and tell ourselves we are great the way we are. God made me this way, we like to say. Wrong; we are broken. If you don't recognize your weakness, you don't understand your need for God. I have sinned mortally. I am deserving of eternal damnation. I know that sounds like a major downer, but this is reality. This is true humility, the truth about me and the truth about God. Yet, if we see this reality as hopelessly bad, it is because we haven't balanced the truth about me with the truth about God. God is good! God is love! I am weak, but God is strong! God in His goodness has redeemed me. In His goodness, He has granted me absolution in the sacrament of Confession. God loves me, and He has saved me. This is the truth.

This also means that I am indebted to God. Jesus Christ sacrificed everything for me, and I owe Him my life. He is faithful, despite my constant backsliding. He has not forsaken me.

Another truth about ourselves that follows: We need help to be good. Despite our good will, we still struggle. This is one of the benefits that addicts bring with them when they take on the Rosary as a lifestyle. Addicts are desperate and have hit rock bottom, seeing the depths of their own depravity. They are very aware of the truth about themselves. Then, when Our Lady picks them up and presents them to her Son, they can be totally committed to her. Not just because she rescued them, but because the addict has learned from experience that if they leave her side even for a day, the demons who enslaved them will return with seven more to accompany them.

The final truth about ourselves: We are good. Many of us are incredibly good. We have a lot of talents and natural abilities. Some are great artists or gifted orators. Some are incredible athletes or blessed with charm and good looks. The truth is, even if we cultivated these qualities, they are a gift from our Creator. Experience teaches us that all that is good has been received as a grace from God. Without the grace of God, we would squander all His blessings. St. Thérèsè of Lisieux never sinned mortally, and yet she was truly humble, because she recognized that her good morals were truly a gift from God. She had received a special preservative grace. Our Lady herself was truly humble, because she recognized that Jesus was her Savior. His saving action on the Cross was applied to her at her conception.

The truly humble person sees clearly and has a healthy distrust of themselves, but a great confidence in God. When the devil comes to accuse you of being bad, it stings. Remember it is only a half truth. Yes, you are weak, but God is good. God is your strength. At the same time, when you see a person committing an act that you deem shameful, remember, but for the grace of God, there go I. This is the truth. We are no better than any other person, and without God's grace, we are all capable of the most shameful acts.

Humility leads to prayer, and prayer, especially the Rosary, increases humility. The Hail Mary reminds us that we are sinners begging Mary for help. The life of Christ is a constant reminder of the goodness of God. What leads me to pray? Humility. What leads me to pray? A distrust of myself and a great confidence in God. There is an idea that sums it up perfectly and is so often repeated, because every saint believed it: We must work as if everything depends on us, but pray as if everything depends on God. Truly humble people work hard, but they drop to their knees before their work to beg God for help, pause during their work to consult with Him, and drop to their knees afterward to thank Him for a job well done. We must bring humility to the Rosary.

As we approach a deeper understanding of the Rosary, we must first pray for grace, because to love Mary and the Rosary is one of the greatest graces. All is grace. We must ask for the grace to pray the Rosary and to love Mary.

Blessed Virgin Mary, we beg of you, please obtain for us the grace to know you and to love you. Please obtain for us the grace to be faithful to your Holy Rosary. Mother Mary, you never fail.

THE FIRST INGREDIENT: SELF-DENIAL

Self-denial is at the heart of the Christian mystery. The great paradox of Christ is: unless you die, you cannot live. The very foundation of the Rosary is an act of self-denial. So many have had the experience of the Rosary being almost painful. Yes. Sometimes it can be painful, because the Rosary is where self-will and self-love go to die. For many, to pray the Rosary when they don't feel like it can be a death, but it is a beautiful death. I will sometimes joke that the Rosary kills me! It kills the worst part of me. Selfish me. Gluttonous me. Slothful me. And there is a death, but the best version of myself emerges.

I will give you one example. I have the habit of praying the Rosary on my way home from work. I've done it over and over, until it is almost second nature to me. It was difficult at first, because I like to listen to music; when I am on my way home from work, I am tired, I am hungry, I want to be left alone. I just want to eat and relax. However, when I pray the Rosary on the way home, it slowly begins to chip away at my selfishness. My will is put to death, and a space is created for me to hear the voice of God.

It is not an earth-shattering revelation, but by the time I get home, I have in my heart a deep conviction of what God wants from me. *How about your wife?* Maybe she is tired. *What is going on in the lives of your children?* Perhaps I should give my middle child some individualized conversation or take the baby outside for a walk. God is making His will clear to me; He wants me to go into my house and give my wife and children attention.

The number one reason we don't do God's will is that we are too preoccupied with our own will. When we pray the Rosary, it costs us fifteen to twenty minutes, but really, we need a good fifteen to twenty minutes anyway to refocus on God and His will. His will is everything. This is the essence of sanctity.

When we sacrifice to do God's will, we have assurance of His providence. When we do God's will, everything is grace-filled. The reason we don't see the mighty hand of God like in the New Testament is because we must first be consumed with accomplishing His will in all things. And this is what happens when we take the leap of self-denial to pray the Rosary. His will begins to permeate our lives. The prayer doesn't change Him, it changes us! Sacrifice is transformed at the Cross. When we unite our little sacrifices to Christ, we begin to step into the saving power of the Resurrection. This is why self-denial is at the foundation of the Rosary. Am I supposed to pray the Rosary at the expense of doing something fun? Something that makes me feel happy? Yes.

This is the paradox of Christianity. Choosing to do God's will actually makes you happy. Christ came for us to have life to the full! You don't become a dud; you become more intensely yourself! And you will find that Our Lady is a real and true mother, who notices her children going out of their way to love, and she cannot help but give true and deep consolations when the time is right.

I am going to continue to use the four Rosaries a day as a recommendation, but all of this applies whether you pray five mysteries a day or twenty. If you pray a Rosary in the morning, one at midday, one in the evening, and one before bed, you are constantly putting yourself to death and constantly starting fresh. The effects of the Rosary on our disposition wear off. We are constantly bombarded with temptations and both small and large irritations throughout the day that wear on us. This is especially true for those who have a diabolical obsession. If we cultivate the habit of praying the Rosary multiple times a day, the devil is beaten back at every turn, and the obsession will be dramatically diminished in time.

St. Louis de Montfort says a sign of spiritual growth is constancy. This means praying when I don't want to pray. An act of sacrifice also helps me to not be so reactive. Often the devil tempts us by appealing to our emotions and passions. By the frequent self-denial found in the Rosary, slowly but surely the will is strengthened. This is especially true when we have the habit of meditating on the Passion of Christ on a daily basis. When we walk with Him on His Way of the Cross, we are strengthened to follow His example and to follow Him. It all starts with self-denial of our will regarding what we want in the moment and making the decision to begin to pray.

Of course, many prayers and activities have elements of self-denial. True, there are many other good and worthy pursuits that aid us in the path to holiness. It is the reliance on self-denial combined with the rest of the ingredients of the Rosary that makes it so powerful. If self-denial is like breaking and tilling the soil of our souls, it is fitting that it is then watered with the Angelic Salutation.

> *When God willed to renew the face of the*
> *earth, he began by sending down on it the*
> *fertilizing rains of the Angelic Salutation.*
> — Mary to St. Dominic[49]

THE SECOND INGREDIENT: VOCAL PRAYER

The vocal prayers of the Rosary are pure theological gold. The essential prayers are truly anointed because not only do they originate from Sacred Scripture, but they originate from the Heart of the Holy Trinity. The Our Father comes from the lips of Our Blessed Lord. The first part of the Hail Mary was delivered by Gabriel, but the message came from God the Father. While it was Elizabeth who proclaimed "Blessed are you amongst women, and blessed is the fruit of your womb," Scripture is clear that she was full of the Holy Spirit when she did so.

The Angelic Salutation does have a prominence and for good reason. When you accept Mary as your mother, at least three essential things take place. First, as a member of the Body of Christ, you resemble Him who accepted Mary as His mother. Second, she begins to actively participate in your formation into another Christ. Third, as a child begins to resemble his mother, so too do you begin to be shaped into an image of Mary. She is the most perfect follower of Christ, and she begins to help you become more like her. She is the only one who can most perfectly say, "It is no longer I who live, but Christ who lives in me."

Pope St. John Paul II says we should enter into the school of Mary. Those precious words, "Hail Mary, full of grace," stir up the Holy Spirit. Those words stir up Our Lady. Those words scatter demons. The first utterance of those words was the turning point of Mary's essential "yes" and a landmark in salvation history. How fitting it is that I first destroy my will by saying no to myself—and that the vehicle of my no to self is the repetition of the words spoken at the moment of history's ultimate yes to God.

The repetitive words of the Hail Mary act almost like a chant that rings out in the background, stirring up the Spirit of the Lord like a storm cloud whirling. The Hail Mary is life giving. The Hail Mary never fails to bring comfort.

I have been to funerals and encountered tragedies where hearts were truly broken, and people's emotions are so raw they can't even meditate. And yet, as the first words of the Rosary begin—"Hail Mary, full of grace"—hope and healing and comfort emerge. Not only are these words the sacred foundation of the New Testament, but they are a Marian invocation. You are calling upon the Holy Mother of God, the Queen of Heaven and Earth. Besides the merits of the words from Scripture and salvation history, add to that the power of calling upon a mother who loves you more than you can imagine. The second half of the Hail Mary is equally profound, calling upon her now and at the hour of our death. The Hail Mary is the greatest assurance that we will have her assistance at the end of our life.

From the vocal prayers alone, you can see we are dealing with power, but this isn't even the Rosary yet. The very heart of the Rosary is the life of Christ.

THE THIRD INGREDIENT: THE LIFE OF CHRIST

It is the fusion of the powerful vocal prayers with the meditation on the life of Christ that sets the Rosary apart from all other prayers.

The life of Christ is the divine fire from which all things flow. The Hail Marys serve to provide the most fertile environment to have a fruitful encounter with Christ. When prayed properly a true encounter with Christ does occur; however, even with the most superficial and imperfect attempts, the inclusion of the life of Our Blessed Lord is beneficial. First, at a catechetical level, through the Rosary a person is given a thorough education and foundation of the major points in the life of Christ. When we make even a feeble grasp at meditation on the mysteries, it will bear fruit, because we are invoking Our Lady, because we are stirring up the spirit with the vocal prayers, and because we have turned our mind to the life of Christ. Even on days of dryness and desolation, here we will receive grace, light, and peace.

Trying to meditate on the life of Christ is fruitful because of an important theological principle: *A grace remembered is a grace renewed.* How many times in the Old Testament are the Israelites instructed to remember the wonders done for them in Egypt, their protection in the desert, and the favors granted to their forefathers? Why? A grace remembered is a grace renewed. For example, to recall the wedding feast of Cana renews in the soul confidence in Our Lady's intercession. To recall Christ's institution of the Eucharist, especially if done daily, ignites an increase of eucharistic faith in His Real Presence and reminds us of the dignity and power of the Mass. To recall the power of Pentecost renews in us Pentecostal fervor and devotion to the Holy Spirit.

Most of this occurs without us even noticing. Similar to an infant at his mother's breast, the baby is only aware that his immediate need is being satisfied, but in addition to his belly being full, he is also being consoled, strengthened, rested, and more deeply bonded to his mother. The same with the Rosary. You might only notice that you are going through the motions, but a lot of growth is happening, which you might not recognize from day to day, but when you look back on your life after a year, there will be major changes. Notice that all of this happens even when the Rosary is prayed poorly.

Even though we see benefits when our prayer feels scattered, we should strive for nothing less than to pray the Rosary using the methods of the saints. With mental prayer, the Rosary becomes like a flaming sword, an impenetrable shield, a tree of life, and a key that unlocks every door in the spiritual life. When the Rosary is prayed well, the person praying is in the presence of God, really entering into the Gospel passage to observe Christ and then really coming into contact with Him.

This is a game changer. Ordinarily you are gaining light and understanding simply because of the words prayed and invocation of the mystery, but using mental prayer you gain insights because you are watching it happen. For example, if you are present at Cana, you watch Mary instruct the waiters to do whatever Jesus tells them to do, and you observe Jesus telling them to go fill the jars with water. It strikes you that in order for Jesus to work the first miracle, more than Mary's intercession is necessary. A third party must be willing to cooperate with Jesus and Mary. Another person has to be willing to do the ridiculous and fill six jars with thirty gallons of water each, when they don't need water, they need wine! You realize that if God is going to work a miracle for you, He needs you to participate. He needs you to do some work. What is He asking you to do? This question arises in your heart. And suddenly the answer hits you. Not in a revelation, but in your soul, you know what He is asking of you.

However, praying the Rosary using mental prayer is far more than that. Imagine you are a priest praying the Third Luminous Mystery, the Proclamation of the Kingdom. You are watching Jesus preach. What does He sound like? You notice His passion. It strikes you that He is preaching as if everything was at stake. He is preaching as if His greatest love is on the line. You feel sad at first, because you don't preach like that, but in mental prayer a theosis happens. By spending time with the One who is the source of all charismatic graces, while you see Jesus preaching, your grace and ability to preach from the heart increase by His example.

However, praying the Rosary using mental prayer is even more than observations and theosis; already that's incredible, but more than that, you speak to Christ, and He speaks back to you! Imagine you are a wife whose husband isn't Catholic. You have been praying for him for years. You are exhausted. You want to quit. You pick up your Rosary. You are on the Fourth Sorrowful Mystery, present on the road as Jesus is carrying His cross. You notice the insults and ingratitude that Jesus is suffering, but you are desperate, and you throw yourself in front of Him, stopping the *Via Dolorosa*, to beg Him to help you.

You tell Him, "Jesus, my husband. I can't keep going!" He looks at you, and you sense His compassion. He kisses the Cross. He reaches for your arm to pull you in. "Let's keep going. For his salvation, and yours." And the two of you carry the Cross. How do you know it is Christ really speaking? Because in the words of St. Teresa of Ávila, "When he speaks, he acts." Jesus says, "Let's keep going," and we know that He suffered even unto death. And suddenly you too are filled with the strength to keep going.

My brothers and sisters, this is the power of the Rosary. Heaven is opened to you. Hell trembles.

Conclusion

> *The extraordinary good that this precious
> devotion has brought to the world is too well
> known. How many souls have been delivered
> from sin by means of the Rosary! How many
> have been converted to a holy life; how many
> have died a good death and are now saved!*
> — St. Alphonsus Liguori[50]

The popes, the great saints, the holiest theologians all agree when it comes to the power and efficacy of the Rosary. Although it is not always easy nor is it always enjoyable, it is effective. No other prayer better touches the Heart of God, reforms the sinner, or destroys vice. No other prayer is more effective in causing virtue and good works to flourish. There is no greater preparation to receive grace from the sacraments than the humble and fervent praying of the Rosary. In it the entire life of Christ is reviewed, and through it Christ is encountered all day, every day. It is simple enough for a child and profound enough for a mystic. Other prayers aren't as effective at giving a balanced spirituality. Only a prayer of divine origin could pull it off.

In the words of Ven. Fulton J. Sheen, "Because the Rosary is both a vocal and a mental prayer, it is one where intellectual elephants may bathe, and the simple birds may also sip."[51] The Rosary is greater than the sum of its parts. It isn't just an act of self-denial; it isn't just a Marian prayer or just a vocal prayer; it isn't just mental prayer. The Rosary is a combination of the most powerful practices in Christendom and it is the Mother of God's favorite tool to help ordinary people to become saints.

I am pleading with you to become apostles of the Rosary. Promote the Rosary. Urge the Rosary. Teach the Rosary. Advertise the Rosary. It is through the Rosary that we can bring countless souls back to Christ from whom they strayed. It is through the Rosary that we can make them lovers of Christ through the mediation of his Mother.

— Servant of God Fr. John Hardon[52]

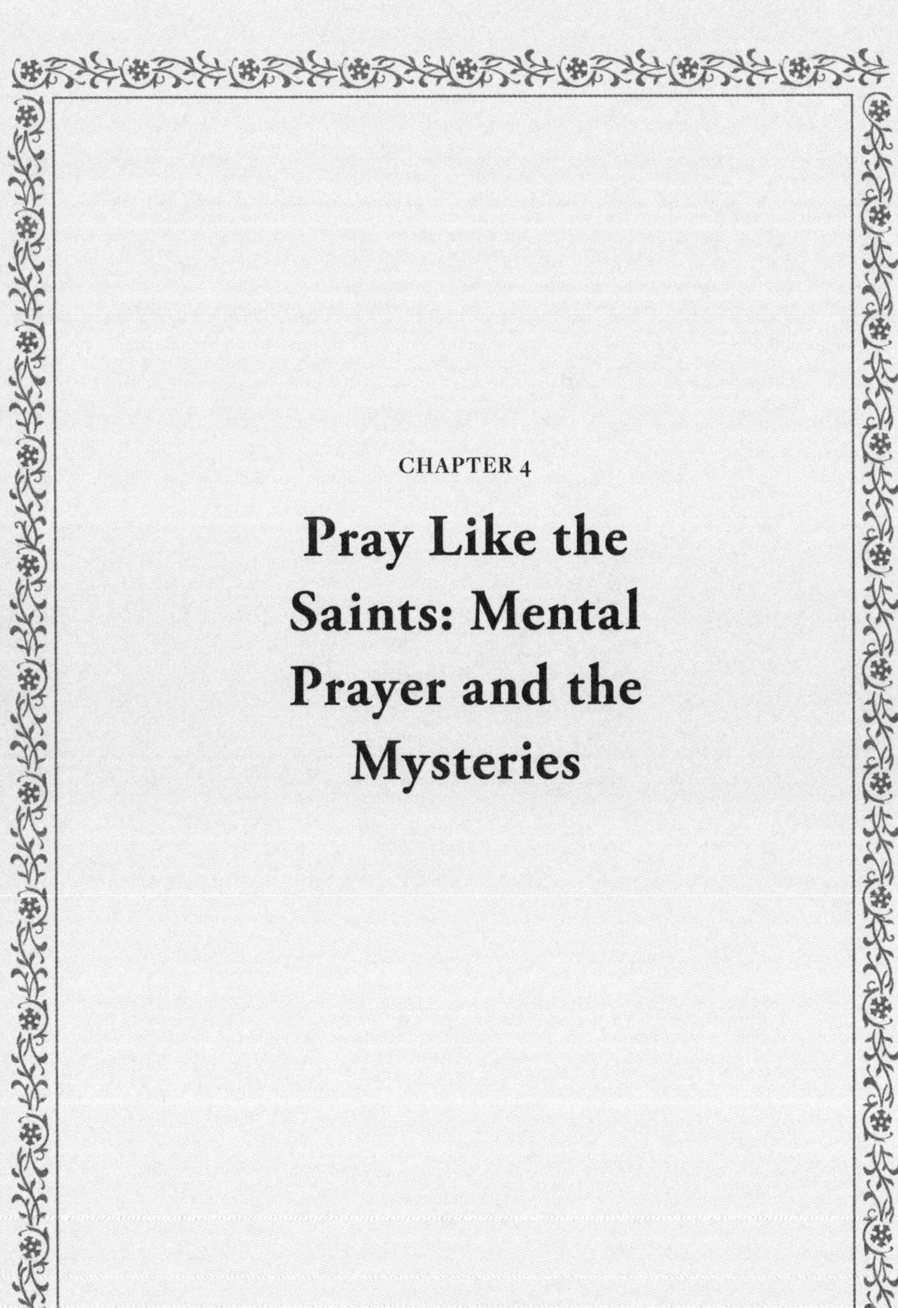

CHAPTER 4

Pray Like the Saints: Mental Prayer and the Mysteries

TWO PEOPLE WALK INTO a church and kneel down. Both are burdened with many worries, but one leaves consoled and the other leaves discouraged. One returns day after day and the other doesn't. What is the difference? One knows how to pray, and the other doesn't.

Learning to apply mental prayer to your Rosary will transform every aspect of your prayer life. St. Teresa of Ávila teaches that mental prayer is the entry point to all the higher forms of prayer. When a person engages in mental prayer, all the divine mysteries are opened to them. St. Alphonsus Liguori teaches that mental prayer is essential for growing in holiness and loving God. He goes so far as to say that God rarely answers those who do not practice mental prayer, and that without the aid of mental prayer, it is morally impossible to avoid sin.

Some of us have no doubt slipped in and out of mental prayer and not realized it. The steps of mental prayer provide a consistent method to encounter Christ, and the secret to praying the Rosary well is to incorporate three essential steps.

HOW THE SAINTS PRAYED

All the greatest saints, popes, and teachers of the Church have urged and encouraged mental prayer. St. Augustine, St. Bernard of Clairvaux, St. Thomas Aquinas, St. Bonaventure, St. Teresa of Ávila, St. John of the Cross, St. Alphonsus Liguori, St. Francis de Sales—all these Doctors of the Church were emphatic: Mental prayer is essential for spiritual growth. We could fill an entire book with quotes on the importance of mental prayer, but I will use just one. The following is from St. Peter of Alcantara, the confessor of St. Teresa of Ávila:

> In mental prayer, the soul is purified from its sins, nourished with charity, confirmed in faith, and strengthened in hope. The mind expands, the affections dilate, the heart is purified, truth becomes evident; temptation is conquered, sadness dispelled; the senses are renovated; drooping powers revive; tepidity ceases; the rust of vices disappear. Out of mental prayer issues forth, like living sparks, those desires of heaven which the soul conceives when inflamed with the fire of divine love. Sublime is the excellence of mental prayer, great are its privileges; to mental prayer heaven is opened; to mental prayer heavenly secrets are manifested and the ear of God is ever attentive.[53]

It is undeniable that mental prayer is a major pillar in the spiritual life. The genius of Our Lady is that she takes the power of mental prayer and *enhances it, simplifies it, and makes it regular* in the lives of all of her children who pray the Rosary.

THE ROSARY ENHANCES MENTAL PRAYER

Earlier we said that self-denial is like breaking ground in the soul. As we pray the Rosary, the flow of constant Hail Marys is like rain watering the soil to make it rich and fertile. The seed—the Word of God—is received and planted in mental prayer. Our Lady, in the Rosary, makes sure that the seed falls on fertile soil and bears fruit thirty-, sixty-, and a hundredfold.

The most fertile place to do mental prayer is in the context of the Rosary, where the Mother of God acts as our mediatrix, advocate, and teacher. St. John Paul II said, "With the Rosary the Christian people *sits at the school of Mary* and is led to contemplate the beauty on the face of Christ and to experience the depths of his love. Through the Rosary, the faithful receive abundant grace, as though from the very hands of the Mother of the Redeemer."[54]

When the Rosary is prayed well, it sets the stage for an encounter with Christ, an encounter in which, through spending time with Jesus and Mary, we are slowly changed, enlightened, strengthened, and renewed.

THE ROSARY SIMPLIFIES MENTAL PRAYER

This method of mental prayer is based on the teachings of three great Doctors of the Church: St. Teresa of Ávila, St. Francis de Sales, and St. Alphonsus Liguori. These three provide the clearest outline for fruitful and effective prayer. They all have essentially the same steps but use different words to describe the approach. Their methods can be summarized in five key steps, and Mary's method in the Rosary reduces the five down to three.

The first step that Mary eliminates is the selection of what you are going to meditate on. The illustrious doctors place great importance on this step, but Our Lady eliminates this entirely. In the school of Mary, the material for contemplation is always the life of Christ. Her primary lesson plan is that we encounter Christ so that in spending time with Him we are transformed into Him. This is a great relief.

The last step of mental prayer is usually called a spiritual bouquet. The great spiritual teachers say to offer Our Lord a bouquet of prayers at the end of our mental prayer in atonement for failures, as a sign of our good will, as a deposit on our good resolutions, and in thanksgiving for graces received. Our Lady again removes this step; in the Rosary, she streamlines this process, and the bouquet we offer to the Lord is a decade of roses offered to Him through her immaculate hands.

The Rosary Makes Mental Prayer a Habit

Most people don't purposefully do any mental prayer. The average Catholic doesn't even know what mental prayer is, but Our Lady makes this a regular practice in all her children's lives. When they begin to pray the Rosary, some people go from no mental prayer to mental prayer twenty times a day! Not even knowing the clear steps, many have experienced moments of consolation and contemplation, simply by going through the motions. "The Rosary is a school of contemplation and silence," according to Pope Benedict XVI.[55]

Sometimes educated people will treat the Rosary as if it is a prayer for simpletons. The opposite is true. According to St. Louis de Montfort, if you wish to attain a high degree of prayer yet remain humble and safe from the traps of the devil, you must be faithful to the Rosary. It is those who pray the Rosary who learn to be masters of prayer.

If you persevere in prayer, Our Lady will intercede and obtain for you all the light you need. Have confidence that she can plunge a soul into divine consolation whenever she sees fit. This regular habit of mental prayer that you will develop by the frequent praying of the Rosary will open every door in the spiritual life. Even if you find it difficult at first, persevere, because you will get better with every Rosary. The only way to get better at prayer is by praying. I promise that because of your frequent habit of mental prayer, three doors will be opened. You will have a better sense of the presence of God between Rosaries; your ability to use mental prayer during the Mass and in the presence of the Blessed Sacrament will increase; and you will be filled with light and strength when all human effort seems to fail.

THREE ESSENTIAL STEPS TO MENTAL PRAYER IN THE ROSARY

Let's look at the three steps that will take your Rosary to the next level, beginning with a detailed explanation of each and then considering how to integrate them seamlessly with the Rosary.

Step 1: Recollection.

The first step to all prayer is to make an act of faith in the presence of God. Sometimes this happens naturally in our day-to-day life, but it is an essential step that is best made deliberately.

The most concrete way to make an act of faith in God's presence is to verbalize it: "God, I believe You are present. You are holding me in existence. You see me. You love me. You are so close. I am literally a temple of the Holy Spirit. I am truly a member of the Body of Christ. Holy God, You are in the very air I breathe. You are so close to me." Making an act of faith like this changes us. Our interior faculties are the intellect and the will, our mind and our heart. By presenting this truth to our minds, the presence of God impacts our hearts.

This becoming aware of the presence of God, we call recollection. Taking a moment to recollect yourself is the way to start all prayer, and it is the secret to making everything a prayer. The saints made great efforts to always be recollected, to live with a sense of the presence of God, not just an awareness of God's divine action but also His living presence within us. This presence of God in our soul cannot be understated.

St. Teresa of Ávila urged, "Let us realize that we have within us a palace of incomparable splendor. Within this palace, is the great King, Whose Kindness has led Him to be your Father; He sits on a throne of priceless value, which is your heart."[56]

Recollection is an act of humility, simply taking a moment to be aware of the truth: God is unimaginably close. See the leaves and the clouds and the seasons; the omnipotence and love of God is everywhere manifested. It is important to regularly make concrete acts of faith in God's presence. It isn't always necessary to use words. There will be times when we are walking in His presence and we simply lift our eyes and hearts to Him.

If we are truly burdened and go to the Church for relief, we must begin by acknowledging the Person we are addressing. We must get on our knees and say, "Jesus, I believe You are really here in the most Blessed Sacrament. I believe You see me. I believe You hear me. I believe You love me." Just as human conversations begin with acknowledging the presence of the person, the same is true in prayer.

When we start our Rosary, we should begin with an act of faith in the presence of God and acknowledge the presence of Mary. We can say in the silence of our hearts, "Blessed Mother, I believe you are with me. I believe you are close to me. I believe you are my mother and you love me and you never take your eyes off me. Blessed Mother, you are the spouse of the Holy Spirit and the mediatrix of every grace I receive. I beg you, help me to pray this Rosary well."

These words are just an example; there is no set formula, and it only takes a moment. The key is that from our heart we acknowledge that she is with us and close to us.

I mentioned that it is fitting to make acts of recollection at natural moments throughout the day, but the same is true when praying. We make an act of recollection before we begin the Rosary and at the natural breaking points, in this case the beginning of a new decade. The goal is that we begin the mystery with a sense that we are close to God, and He sees us. That is it. Step 1 is easy. What I have described takes seconds, but makes all the difference.

Step 2: Consideration.

The second step of mental prayer is to consider the subject matter. We use our intellect and imagination to reflect on some aspect of the life of Christ.

The goal of the consideration (or meditation) is to stir up love and put us in contact with God. According to St. Teresa of Ávila and St. Francis de Sales, this is best done by imagining the mystery as if we are really present at the particular scene. So, if you are praying the Crucifixion of Christ, try and behold this as if you are standing at the foot of the Cross. You can pick any aspect of the Crucifixion to focus on. All of it is fruitful. Imagine the feet of Christ with a nail piercing them and blood dripping out. Imagine Our Lady standing near the Cross of Christ, tears running down her face. Spending time here changes us.

How long do we consider the mystery? Ideally until it makes an impression on us, until something strikes us or moves us. This will provide fuel for our conversation with Christ. But practically, how long do we ponder the mystery? My personal recommendation is twenty to thirty seconds. This is a reasonable effort within the context of a Rosary, but there is no time limit. Some days you might have a very pressing intention, and you really need to hear from the Lord about a particular situation, and you don't want to rush the conversation. Or, perhaps you are in the mystery, and Christ is really taking over and pouring out His Spirit upon you. Don't interrupt and say, "Well Lord, it's been thirty seconds, Your time is up." A conversation with Christ is the endgame.

Not everybody has the same capacity for imagination, and depending on the day and your disposition, this might be easy or difficult, but it is the best way, and so we should make an effort. It doesn't always need to be a vivid imagining. Even if your mind is scattered and you can only recall facts about the mystery, this will suffice. It might be just enough to provide you with reflection. So, for example, we may not be able to visualize Mary visiting her cousin Elizabeth, but just by thinking of it, we can reflect that, upon Mary's greeting, Elizabeth was filled with the Holy Spirit. That reflection is enough to spark a conversation: "Blessed Mother, please speak to me. I need to hear your voice. Holy Spirit, fill me like St. Elizabeth." An accurate image isn't as essential as truly considering what is happening.

St. Teresa of Ávila encourages people who suffer from a poor imagination to take advantage of pictures or even written descriptions or meditations. We are fortunate to have the benefit of recalling things we have seen in movies and an abundance of religious art. Don't be afraid to draw on these resources.

Why is giving some time to consideration so essential? If a person never takes time to consider the life of Jesus Christ, how can they know Him? Think of the frustrated parent telling a teenager, "God loves you. He suffered for you." The parent truly believes it, but the child doesn't care. What is the difference? Maybe the parent has spent a lot of time considering the Passion of Christ, visualizing it, and truly encountering Christ there in prayer. If a person never prayerfully considers Christ and His life, not only can they not know Him, but they can't love Him or accept His love.

Remember, our interior faculties are the intellect and the will. The will is essentially a blind faculty. We must feed our intellect truths to consider, and this guides our will.

One of my favorite films to watch during Lent is *The Passion of the Christ*. So many people were deeply moved by this film and many had conversion experiences. Why? People may have heard, "Jesus loves you. Jesus died for you," but this was the first time it entered the imagination. For many people that particular movie was a very long mental prayer. Spending this prolonged time in consideration of His Passion leads us to cry out, "My Lord and my God, forgive me for my sins." I often use scenes from such films as fuel for meditation during the Rosary.

At the start of every decade, we announce the mystery and then use our intellect to ponder some truth, consider some detail, and ideally imagine the mystery as if we are present. That is the goal. Even if we fail at forming an image, that doesn't mean the prayer is fruitless. St. Francis de Sales teaches that even if we spend the entire time in prayer fighting off distraction, consider that time well spent. Prayer isn't about feelings. Grace is working in us, most especially when we pray in times of dryness and distraction. That being said, implementing these concrete steps will result in more frequent moments of encounter, and even our dry spells will be more satisfying than our previous method of prayer.

I will make two major recommendations here. First, I always try to end my consideration by looking into the eyes of Christ or His Blessed Mother in that particular mystery. Looking into His eyes reinforces that Christ is present, and He is close. The eyes are often described as the gateway to the soul, and when we look into the eyes of a person we love or who loves us, we can communicate deep truths without saying a single word. You will find that by simply looking into Christ's eyes, on the Way of the Cross for example, He communicates that He sees you, that He loves you, and many other beautiful sentiments of conviction and encouragement.

Second, when using imagination to behold the scene as if truly present, I personally start my consideration with something that I have seen before. For example, when praying the Third Joyful Mystery, I imagine I am holding baby Jesus. I look at His fat baby feet. Have you ever put your finger in a baby's hand? Use that moment of experience of having held a baby to be the fuel for your prayer and marvel that the Creator of the universe, He who holds us in existence, has humbled Himself to be held in your arms.

Truly there is great freedom. St. Francis de Sales says we can be like bees who go from flower to flower looking for pollen. Any aspect of the mystery can be sought, as long as it is insightful for us. He even gives permission to imagine the mystery as if it is happening in the place where we are. For example, if we are praying in a chapel, imagine if the mystery of Pentecost was taking place in that very room. If you are praying outside, you can look to the sky as you consider Jesus' Ascension into Heaven. There is freedom. This is the key. During our consideration, all the greatest saints encourage us to strive to use our imagination, which will provide fuel for our encounter with Christ in conversation.

Step 3: Conversation.

We have done so much to stir up the Holy Spirit. We have placed ourselves in the presence of God, we have incessantly called upon Mary, and then we go to the most fertile place in the world to have a conversation with Christ: We literally enter the Gospel. The Gospels are the inspired Word of God, and in them, we are immersed in the presence of the Holy Spirit. All of this so that we can have a conversation with Christ.

The following is an example of a consideration and then a sample conversation with Christ.

We can consider the Scourging at the Pillar. Imagine a three-foot stone pillar at the center of a courtyard. Christ's hands are cuffed to the top of the pillar, and Jesus is lying on the ground. There are no Roman soldiers anywhere. His hands and arms are covered in blood. His back and legs are completely shredded from lashings. There is blood pooled beneath Him. His hair is wet and matted. With all His strength, He lifts His head to look at you. You look into His eyes. Now begins the conversation. Speak to Jesus from your heart. "My Lord and my God. I am sorry. Have pity on me." Then you transition to what is on your heart. Poor out to Him your burdens. Beg Him for what it is that you long for. This is the height of prayer: a heart-to-heart conversation with your God.

St. Bonaventure says, "When we pray, the voice of the heart is heard more than the proceedings from the mouth." Petition Jesus concerning whatever is on your heart. St. Alphonsus says that petitioning, begging Jesus, is an essential element of prayer. The ordinary means for receiving grace is to ask. So in the Rosary, at every decade, enter into this conversation with Christ. Yes, continue to consider the mystery. In light of that mystery and in the presence of that mystery, make your requests known.

I will remind you of the quote from St. Alphonsus: "God rarely answers those who do not use mental prayer." Why? Because in mental prayer we don't just call to mind all the ways God has loved us. We encounter the love of God. In light of His divine life, we speak to Him from our hearts. These aren't blind petitions thrown up to whoever will hear us. These are heartfelt encounters with Jesus Christ, offered to God the Father and fueled by humility and confidence.

This isn't over yet. Step 3 is just getting started. I promise this all happens faster and more seamlessly than I can describe, because truly one thing leads to another. The conversation has just begun, because so far only you have done the speaking. Now you must wait for God to speak. The God who spoke the world into existence now speaks to you, but first you must pause. So far you have controlled the process. So far it has been a monologue and an exercise of your imagination. Now you must let go, be still, and allow God to speak back to you. Look into His eyes. He doesn't need words. "He speaks clearly to the heart when we beg Him from our heart to do so," says St. Teresa of Ávila. "Soon after we have begun to force ourselves to remain near the Lord, He will give us indications that He heard us."[57]

This is the secret to mental prayer, because what begins in the mind now moves to the heart. Christ looks at you from the pillar and says, "I love you. Be strong. Keep going. Sacrifice. Trust." Although this is happening in the imagination, the heart is moved. You are convicted. This interior conviction is the action of God. Your Rosary will be like a line between your heart and God's Heart. You will soon be turning to your Rosary when you want to know what to do. A question or an important decision will have to be made, and in time, you will first run to the Rosary to hear from Our Blessed Lord your course of action. You won't necessarily get a divine revelation, but in the depth of your soul, you will know what needs to be done, and you will have the conviction and strength to do it. We will touch on this interior action and discuss how to recognize God's voice more in the section on spiritual warfare and the discernment of spirits. For now, I give you these words of St. Alphonsus, which echo the sentiments of St. Teresa of Ávila:

> He does not, indeed, make Himself heard in any voice that reaches your ears, but in a voice that you can well perceive.... He will then speak to you by such inspirations, such interior lights, such manifestations of His goodness, such sweet touches in your heart, such tokens of forgiveness, such experience of peace, such hopes of heaven, such rejoicing within you ... in a word, such voices of love—as are well understood by those souls whom He loves, and who seek for nothing but Himself alone.[58]

My brothers and sisters, be convinced that God wants to speak with you. Conversation with Christ is the heart of prayer. Not everybody is gifted with a great imagination, but we all have a heart. We can love Christ and speak to Him. If you can pour out your heart to Him, He is far more generous and will pour out His Heart to you. This is the image of the Sacred Heart: His Heart bleeds and suffers for your love. Have confidence in Christ and have confidence in Mary's intercession.

I have quoted from three heavyweight Doctors of the Church: St. Teresa of Ávila, St. Francis de Sales, and St. Alphonsus. I have selected these three because, not only are they masters of the spiritual life and have reached the greatest heights of prayer, but because each one prayed all the mysteries of the Rosary every day. These spiritual giants clung to the Rosary as a foundation of the spiritual life and an anchor in turbulent times. With their intercession, may we do the same.

Applying These Principles to the Rosary: A Thirty-Second Secret

Recollection. Consideration. Conversation. An easy acronym to remember is RCC, which calls to mind Roman Catholic Church. This is the thirty-second secret that will radically change the power of your Rosary.

Just so that we are clear about the simplicity of this process, we will review it one more time in the context of the Rosary. Suppose we are praying the Fifth Joyful Mystery: The Finding of the Child Jesus after He was lost for three days. We interiorly recollect ourselves. From the heart we can say, "Blessed Mother, I believe you are with me." Or, we can imagine her in front of us. Then we will consider the mystery. Take a moment to try and behold the scene as if you are present. Imagine what Mary looks like. She is frantic. She lost her Son. She lost God! Can you imagine the torment and anxiety of having lost your child and that Child is also the Savior of the world? As she frantically searches for three days, you can walk with her. Help her search for Jesus. Once you have a sense of the scene and an impression is made on your heart, relate your current situation to hers. Speak to her from your heart about your problems.

Perhaps one of your children has left the Faith. "Blessed Mother, ease my anxiety. Help my daughter to find Jesus in the Catholic Church just as you found Him in the temple. Lord Jesus, help my daughter to hear your teaching just as the scholars of the law heard you." Of course I am using human language, but you communicate from the heart. I focused on Mary's anxiety, but there is so much you could focus on. You might turn your attention to the feelings of St. Joseph. You could spend time in consideration with Jesus in the temple. What would it have been like to hear the young Jesus preaching? Whatever you can relate to will work. After giving it a good effort and conversing with Jesus, Mary, or St. Joseph, you begin the vocal prayer.

During the vocal prayer you have freedom. Usually, if your mental prayer is fruitful, there is a lingering of the mystery still on your mind. The image or the conversation will still be heavy on your heart. It is okay if you focus more on the mystery than on the words pronounced. It could be that your consideration was dry and getting the words out is all you can do. That is also fine.

Remember that prayer is a grace, a gift. We must be humble. "Lord, I am new to this!" It is wise to invoke the Holy Spirit before praying or even during prayer if we are struggling. Holy Spirit, help me to pray. Guardian Angel, help me to pray. Dryness in prayer is a normal part of the human condition. We go through cycles, with times of desolation and times of consolation and comfort. Constancy and perseverance in prayer are key. God resists no one that perseveres.

> *Even if you have to fight distractions all through*
> *your whole Rosary, be sure to fight well, arms*
> *in hand: that is to say, do not stop your Rosary*
> *even if it is hard to say and you have no sensible*
> *devotion. It is a terrible battle, I know, but*
> *one that is profitable to the faithful soul.*
> — St. Louis De Montfort[59]

FINAL REMARKS ON MENTAL PRAYER

> *By the efficacy of mental prayer, temptation*
> *is banished, sadness is driven away, and*
> *the flame of divine love is intensified.*
> — St. Laurence Justinian[60]

Step 1: Recollection — "God, You are here."
Step 2: Consideration — Enter the mystery.
Step 3: Conversation — Speak from the heart, then listen.

Recollection, Consideration, Conversation. Notice, I was very careful not to use the word *meditation*. If you were to look up the writings of the great saints on mental prayer, you would find that they used the terms *mental prayer* and *meditation* synonymously. Within the same paragraph, they would use the word interchangeably. This is how mental prayer has been lost to modern generations. We hear "meditate on the mysteries," and we reduce that to a quick and dry examination. What meditation really means is mental prayer, to enter into the mystery and examine it as one who is present, and then to have an encounter with God there, speaking to Him from our heart. Keep this in mind when reading ancient texts and the writings of the saints. The entire goal of all prayer is an encounter with God, never a dry exercise.

I used the example of the Scourging at the Pillar earlier because that was the favorite consideration of St. Teresa of Ávila. It made an impression on her quickly, and she could more easily enter into a heart-to-heart conversation with Christ. This is what will happen to you because of your mental prayer in the Rosary. You are building up an arsenal of fruitful "meditations" that you can call upon at any moment to enter into a conversation with Christ. For me, the Crucifixion of Christ is where I hear the voice of Jesus the clearest. Moments of consolation in mental prayer are similar to a well of water. Now that I have identified where the water is, I can easily go back to that well to get more to drink.

This is particularly important at Mass. When we are at Mass, our eyes fail us. We are really and truly present at the one Crucifixion of Christ, and we are present at the heavenly liturgy; all of this is hidden to our eyes, but because of this frequent habit of mental prayer, during the Mass we can easily close our eyes and see with the eyes of the soul what is really happening. I can easily call to mind the Crucifixion, which I have visited daily in my Rosary, and I can now see the Mass for what it really is. This opens my soul to receive an ocean of grace that I wouldn't otherwise receive without this mental reflection.

Lastly, because of your habit of mental prayer during the Rosary, you will find that this presence of Jesus and Mary spills out in your daily activities. You can visualize the Virgin Mary going with you on a walk and have a heart-to-heart conversation with her. You can visualize Jesus sitting in the passenger seat of your car.

This is the beauty of mental prayer: God really is present, and we use the intellect God gave us to help realize it. This is the method of praying like the saints.

> *The Devil knows that he has lost the soul that*
> *perseveringly practices mental prayer.*
>
> — St. Teresa of Ávila[61]

CHAPTER 5

Spiritual Warfare and the Holy Rosary

The Rosary, a succession of Hail Marys with which we can strike, conquer, and destroy all of Hell's demons.
— St. John Bosco[62]

T HERE IS A GREAT cosmic battle that rages all around us, but the battle is not between God and the devil. It isn't the forces of Heaven versus the forces of Hell. The power of God is infinite. All of Hell cannot lift a finger against God. This battle is being waged on earth, by men. In the Garden, God declared that the enmity is between the serpent and the woman, between the devil's offspring and hers.

In the twelfth chapter of the book of Revelation, we read that the dragon goes off to make war against the woman and her offspring. Mary is that woman. We are her offspring, "those who keep God's commandments and bear witness to Jesus" (See Rev. 12:17).

Mary is utterly victorious in this spiritual combat. She is humble and totally dependent upon God, His will, and His grace. Our Lord elevated her to be the Queen of the Angels. From the moment of her conception, Mary has always utterly humiliated Satan.

In Mary's fourth apparition at Lourdes, St. Bernadette was in the grotto when suddenly she heard a terrible noise coming from the river behind her. It was as if all of Hell was emptied out and legions of demons were rushing the grotto, attempting to scare Bernadette away! There were terrible shouts and screams, "Go away! Begone! Leave!" Bernadette made the move that all children of Mary should make when we are under attack. She looked to the Virgin Mary. Bernadette said that Mary simply looked in the direction of the tumult. Instantaneously, with a single glance, all of Hell was driven back in fright.

This is the power of Mary. This is the victory of Christ. Mary is the Queen of Heaven and Earth, and all obey. Hell doesn't stand a chance. Yet we are at war. Every person is at war against the world, the flesh, and the devil.

In this chapter, we will discuss valuable lessons about spiritual warfare and the Rosary. This isn't a scary chapter but rather one of great liberation and freedom. Spiritual warfare isn't about extraordinary diabolical activity, although we will touch on that out of necessity, but rather it is something far more practical and relevant that plays out in the ordinary and mundane of day-to-day life. Just as in the Rosary we can hear the voice of God and follow it, so we must learn to hear the voice of the enemy and reject it.

> *The Rosary is a powerful weapon to put the demons*
> *to flight, to preserve the integrity of life, to acquire*
> *virtue more easily, and in a word to attain true peace.*
>
> — Pope Pius XI[63]

THE SNARES OF THE DEVIL VERSUS THE CHILDREN OF MARY

> *Some people are so foolish that they think they can go*
> *through life without the help of the Blessed Mother.*
> *Love the Madonna and pray the Rosary, for her Rosary*
> *is the weapon against the evils of the world. All graces*
> *given by God pass through the Blessed Mother.*
>
> — St. Padre Pio[64]

The pure hatred of Satan and the fallen angels is indescribable in human words. Their deepest longing is the utter destruction and eternal torment of every human soul. The fallen angels never sleep, but spend their "Hell on earth" working to encourage man's self-destruction. They want us to be like them, to reject God and His will. And so, they work both to pervert the culture and to pervert every individual specifically, enticing them to choose their own damnation and to die in mortal sin. These demons are always watching, always plotting, and strategically tempting. As the *Catechism of the Catholic Church* states, "This dramatic situation of the whole world, which is in the power of the evil one, makes man's life a battle: The whole of man's history has been the story of dour combat with the powers of evil."[65]

In the midst of this, we must remember Our Lady's words to St. Dominic: "In this type of war the battering ram is the Angelic Psalter." The Hail Mary may be a rose at the feet of Mary, but it is a weapon against the devil. Fr. Gabriel Amorth, the chief exorcist of Rome during the pontificate of St. John Paul II, said that the Hail Mary is like a piercing blow to the head of the devil.

This is theologically accurate. In the book of Genesis, God the Father foretold that the serpent's head would be crushed. It was the words "Hail Mary, full of grace" that marked the beginning of the end for Satan. Now and forever, the Hail Mary will be like a humiliating blow to the proud intellect of the demons. Despite all his scheming and plotting to ruin men, the devil can never accurately calculate the power of humility, prayer, and the actions of the Virgin Mary.

When an individual chooses to pray the Rosary, not only does he rain down blows upon the enemy of souls, but he gives permission for Mary to take an active role in his life. Like at the wedding at Cana, Mary takes the initiative to intercede in ways we don't even know we need. One of my favorite novenas and titles for Mary is "Undoer of Knots." When we pray the Rosary, Our Lady looks at the knots in our lives and begins to unravel our messes. She also looks at the snares the devil has set up, and she doesn't just remove them but often uses them against him. The Rosary destroys the plots of the devil. When a temptation arises, if we have recourse to Mary, we will receive all the necessary assistance to overcome the temptation. What the enemy destined for our downfall, the Mother of God uses for our sanctification. God has given us free will; we must cry out to Our Mother and place ourselves under her care.

The rosary is so powerful that just holding it out of devotion does great good. When a Christian picks up the rosary with confidence, this act alone causes demons to tremble. In our hands we have all the mysteries of the lives of Jesus and Mary. The very sound the beads make is like a bell reminding the demons of their doom. Always carry a rosary with you.

> *The Rosary is a weapon in our hands with*
> *which we can overcome the devil's attacks.*
> — St. Padre Pio[66]

THE ROSARY AND THE FAMILY

For all their plotting and scheming to destroy souls, the demons have a special plot and scheme to destroy the family. When a man and a woman come together in Holy Matrimony and use their sexuality in an ordered way, they are living images of the Holy Trinity. So the devil hates the family, because he sees in the family the image of God.

We live in a very challenging time. The culture has been engineered to make it extremely easy to be perverted and addicted from a young age. So many young people are raised without God. Sadly, even in devout families, children are easily corrupted by the world. Things are so dark that often parents and educators feel hopeless, but I promise there is hope. Sr. Lucia of Fatima foretold, "The decisive battle will be over Marriage and the Family — but do not be afraid because Our Lady has already crushed his head."[67] Where sin abounds, grace abounds all the more. In Mary there is victory, but we must engage in the battle with her.

Mary told Bl. Alan that whoever prays her Rosary is her true child and under her special protection. Mary takes her role as mother very seriously. Mary protects her children. The charism of Our Lady is to crush the head of the serpent. If a member of the family were to invite sin into the home by some hidden means, Our Lady would make sure that this hidden serpent is brought to light, is confronted head-on, and is crushed. The power of the family Rosary destroys the plots of the devil. Even in families that are not unified in faith, if only one person in the family will fully commit to the Rosary, the work of the devil will begin to unravel. Time and time again, when a person gives himself fully over to the Rosary, grace begins to flow into the family, and one by one the family members are converted. How many times do we hear of a fallen relative converting because of the persistent prayers of a loved one? Let us be that instrument!

Mothers and fathers, you must pray the Rosary for your children. You must teach them the Rosary and get them in the habit of praying it from the youngest age, so their mind and their imagination may be filled with Christ. We don't need a revelation from a saint or an exorcist to prove to us that the devil has his sights set on corrupting the purity of the youth. Everywhere you look, we see infidelity and sexual promiscuity being promoted in movies, games, and music. The battle has breached our front door, and it is now in our pockets. We must fight for the souls of our children. If we arm them with the habit of the Rosary, when the world, the flesh, and the devil begin to rage against them, Our Lady will come to their rescue.

I have spent a lot of time in youth ministry and have seen many stories of youth overcoming the temptations of the world to live lives of great virtue. In my experience, when families have the habit of the family Rosary, the kids become faithful Catholics and stand out for their piety. Even in the rare case that a family member goes astray, we should have great confidence they will find their way back. Prayer and sacrifice are our shields and our weapons, which have never been known to fail.

Fathers especially must be men of prayer and sacrifice. When the father takes up his position as the leader of the family, the grace flows down in abundance to the other members. Remember the influence that St. John Paul II's father had on him. It wasn't just seeing his father's good example that benefited young Karol Wojtyla. The efficacious prayers of his father protected Karol and nourished him with grace. This culture and all of Hell is nothing compared to the grace of God obtained by parents who are prayer warriors. Your family can thrive and become a beacon of light in the darkness. Mary never loses. The children of Mary can and will go from victory to victory, but the children of Mary must be children of the Rosary.

Have extraordinary trust in the Rosary, which when prayed well, with humility and confidence, makes a person almost invincible. Every attack of the enemy turns for your greatest good and his greater humiliation. The devil's only recourse is to do everything in his power to get you to stop praying the Rosary, so be assured that whoever resolves to pray the Rosary, the devil will seek to discourage. His primary tactics will be through distractions, desolations, and negative thoughts. He will use a voice that sounds a lot like yours. When you are tired, he will whisper, "It's late. You really need your rest." When you pray, he will flood your mind with distractions and afterward whisper, "That was terribly prayed. You aren't good at this. Mary will never accept a prayer like that." You must understand that the evil spirits are intellectual creatures, and they are fighting for our mind. They know that if we persevere in the Rosary, they will lose their influence on us. The meditation on the life of Christ that happens in the intellect is like a raging fire that drives back the forces of the enemy.

So many people's minds have been perverted and damaged, and the life of Christ is a rebuke to these disordered thoughts. When His life is reviewed over and over, it restores order to the mind and tranquility to the heart. Have confidence! The Rosary works. Have humility! We need the help of Mary. The devil is helpless against her. In a certain sense, the devil hates Mary more than he hates God. It is one thing to be put to shame by God who is omnipotent, but for the proudest creature to be defeated by the humblest girl is eternal torment. Humility is the key to the Rosary and overcoming the devil's temptations to get you to quit.

Don't be discouraged by any distraction. Don't be discouraged if you feel like your prayer is poorly done. In humility say to Mary, "Please accept this. This is the best I can do." Our Lady accepts all prayers. She accepts the Rosary and gives you grace even if you spent the entire time fighting distractions. The devil is a legalist and will argue that you didn't pray it well enough, but to Hell with him, literally. Mary is a mother. She will take your poor prayers and present them to the Father.

If you become a person who lives by the Rosary, you will rarely think about "spiritual warfare" because you have entrusted everything to Mary. Your only preoccupation will be with the will of God and spending time with Jesus and Mary in prayer. In trials, everywhere you look, you will only see Mary.

YOUR GUARDIAN ANGEL AND THE ROSARY

Although the fallen angels have a great fear of Mary and despise her Rosary, the Holy Angels of God have the greatest love for their queen. The Holy Angels provide a special protection and ministry to those who pray the Rosary and are more active in the lives of those who have a devotion to them. The saints teach us that if we want to see the action of our guardian angels, it is important to foster this relationship by praying to them and calling upon them frequently. Like God and His Holy Mother, the angels do not impose their assistance on anyone. Allow me to give you two insights that will forever impact the way you relate to the angels.

First, the greater your reliance upon Mary, the Queen of Angels, the more you will see their activity in your life. So, although it is true if we have a greater devotion to the angels, we will see their activity more, it is also true that the greater our love and devotion to Mary, the more we will see the activity of the Holy Angels. Think of the saints who had extraordinary encounters with their guardian angels, such as St. Padre Pio, St. Gemma Galgani, and St. John Bosco, just to name a few. They were all children of the Rosary.

St. John Bosco was gifted with prophetic dreams and visions where his guardian angel would act as his guide and teacher. On several occasions his guardian angel took the form of a great dog that rescued him from kidnappers and guarded his life. St. John Bosco was completely in love with the Virgin Mary and prayed the entire Rosary every day.

In the life of St. Gemma Galgani, her guardian angel was a true friend and companion. Her guardian angel would give her instructions in the spiritual life and run special errands for her. St. Gemma Galgani was a great lover of the Virgin Mary and prayed the entire Rosary every day.

St. Padre Pio was perhaps the most famous of all, for having daily discourses and frequent encounters with not just his own guardian angel but the angels of other people! He would tell people, "If you need anything, send me your guardian angel!" On many occasions Padre Pio would send his guardian angel to people to offer assistance and consolation. Padre Pio was a great lover of the Virgin Mary and prayed the entire Rosary several times a day, as often as possible. The correlation between praying the Rosary and the ministry of the angels is direct. One leads to the other.

Why do we see a correlation between guardian angels and the Rosary? For many reasons. First and foremost, those who pray the Rosary cry out to the Mother of God. Mary loves her children with an indescribable love, and she has under her command all the angels in Heaven to help her accomplish God's designs. If her child is in trouble, what mother wouldn't send a legion of angels to come to the aid of her little one? Just as God delights in using the angels as secondary causes, the Virgin Mother delights in sending the Holy Angels to do good for her children. The angels played a constant role in the life and ministry of Jesus Christ her Son, so it is fitting that we who have given our entire lives to Mary, for her to make us other Christs, would have the influence of the angels during our entire lives also.

The angels love the Rosary because they love the Angelic Salutation. When we repeat the words of St. Gabriel, just as it causes the demons in Hell to tremble, the Hail Mary inflames the Holy Angels with love and zeal. Remember the principle we discussed earlier, a grace remembered is a grace renewed. When we have a robust review of the life of Christ by praying the entire Rosary, we encounter the frequent role of the angels in the economy of salvation. At every major point in the lives of Christ, Joseph, and Mary, and in the life of the Church, we encounter the angels.

Think of just the early life of Christ. At the Annunciation, we encounter Gabriel. The angel appears to Zechariah. St. Joseph takes Mary into his home at the message of an angel. The angels appear to the shepherds during the Nativity, and later angels warn Joseph to flee to Egypt. When you pray the Rosary, your faith in the angels increases, and their noticeable activity in our lives increases. They are active even in the faithless, but they often go unnoticed.

We are not all promised that we will see our angel in a visible way like some of the great mystics, but we can be confident that, as result of our frequent recitation of the Rosary, we will see the hand of our guardian angel more frequently. This brings us to the second insight concerning the Holy Angels: The principal driving factor of sanctity is the will of God.

Your guardian angel was created by God for one reason, which is to help you to do the will of God. Just as the fallen angels want you to become like them by rejecting God and His will, the Holy Angels want you to become like them by accepting God and His will. Yes, they will guard and protect you, but above all else they want to help you accomplish one thing, the will of God.

This is the essence of sanctity, for you, your angel, and the Virgin Mary: union with the will of God. Set the will of God as the sole principle of your life, and with the Rosary as your foundation, it will be easy to see the angels' influence. The angels will assist you to do God's will and will intervene when, through human frailty, you get sidetracked.

Imagine that it is your grandmother's birthday. The reminder came to you in prayer, and you must call your grandmother and do it immediately or you will forget. Suddenly the doorbell rings, and it is a friend who arrives unexpectedly and out of excitement, through no fault of your own, you lose track of your resolution. Your friend invites you to lunch and you agree. On the way out the door, you grab your keys, and they suddenly drop from your hand. You pick them up, but again they drop from your hands. This time it almost feels like the keys were slapped from your hands. That's unusual. You pause, and it hits you. "Wait. Before we go, I need to call my grandmother!"

St. John Paul II famously said, "In the designs of Providence there are no mere coincidences."[68] In situations like these odd providences, an illumination of the intellect and a sudden understanding, we can't be positive that it was our angel, but we can be sure it was from God. These moments of clarity and serendipitous occurrences are common in the lives of those that pray the Rosary. Note that the angels will ordinarily not assist you when you knowingly choose evil. This type of intervention usually only occurs when you have made a resolution to do God's will.

Some see ordinary events, but with the eyes of faith that are opened during the Rosary, the extraordinary can be found even in the ordinary. As you take an active role in your faith, your angel will match your efforts. When we pray the Rosary, we don't just give Mary permission to protect us from bad angels; we give Mary and our angels permission to help us to be good.

This simply doesn't happen for those that don't have recourse to Mary. Heaven honors our free will, and like the Holy Angels, we may use our freedom to choose God's will. I hope you see the next obvious question. If God's will is so important, how do I know God's will? There is no greater devotion for the discernment of spirits than praying the Holy Rosary.

THE DISCERNMENT OF SPIRITS AND THE GLORY OF THE ROSARY

In this section, we are going to cover one of the most important topics in the spiritual life. To become the person God created you to be and to accomplish His specific will for you is the goal of life and the greatest adventure. It is essential that we discern God's will with and through Mary, because truly she is our safeguard on this journey, as St. Louis de Montfort attested: "Can a child obedient to Mary go astray in the paths to eternity? 'If you follow Her,' says St. Bernard, 'you cannot wander from the road.' Where the guidance of Mary is, neither the evil spirit with his illusions, nor heretics with their subtleties, can ever come."[69]

Consistently differentiating between the voice of God and the voice of the devil in prayer is essential. The discernment of spirits is one of the most valuable tools in our spiritual arsenal. On this topic, we will be taking insights from the great spiritual master, St. Ignatius of Loyola. It should be noted that St. Ignatius was a fervent devotee of the Virgin Mary and prayed the entire Rosary every day. After reviewing the basics, we will see how the Rosary is the greatest prayer for discerning the will of God.

A person living in mortal sin has rejected God and is under the dominion of the devil, and the devil wants to keep him stuck in this state. So the voice of the evil spirit whispers excuses, encourages complacency, and wants the person to feel a false sense of security living in sin. The devil wants to keep a person in mortal sin from "waking up." God, on the other hand, wants to shake him free from this spell. The voice of the good spirit makes him feel guilty, restless, and agitated. God inspires thoughts of "I need to change. I can't keep living like this." God's voice is a call to wake us up. A person living in mortal sin is offered a choice, but if he feels no need to change, this is truly a bad situation. In their pride, sinners often don't cry out for help.

Considering we are deep into a book on the Rosary, I presume you love God and want to be good. So we will now focus on guidelines of discernment for those going from a desire to be good to a continual desire to be better.

The voice of God, the Blessed Mother, the saints, or your guardian angel, we will call the "good spirit." The interior voice of good cheers you on, pushes you forward, and brings peace into the soul when you are troubled. "You can do this. I am with you." The voice of the good spirit convicts us to follow the commandments and grow in virtue. Generally, any deep interior movements or increase in faith, hope, or love are considered the voice of the good spirit. These voices will convict us if we need correction, and there is strength behind them. We are left feeling stronger. This is interesting, because even when we are being called to something difficult and possibly unpopular, there is peace about our resolution. It's like a sports coach pushing us. When we experience the movements to be good, we call these interior convictions a consolation. Remember that word, consolation.

When I say, "the voice of God," I do not mean an audible voice or an internal voice in your head. I am talking about a movement of the soul, a conviction in the conscience, or an illumination of the intellect. The voice of God is often "felt" as a deep conviction in the heart or a sudden understanding in the mind about a given situation or question. This is God speaking. It is easy to deceive ourselves with self-love and try to impose our will on the will of God by manipulating our interior monologue. The voice of God is a movement of the soul, but we can and should put that movement into words.

A simple example: You see an older lady crossing the street, and you notice that she drops her wallet. You experience a tugging on the heart urging you to go pick up the wallet and return it to her. You don't hear words but feel a tug, and if you could give that tug words, they would be, "Help this woman." This tug is a consolation, a conviction to be good. These times of consolation are the times we make commitments and resolutions, because these are from God. While reading this book, you may feel a strong conviction to pray the family Rosary, go to Confession, or to give up a vice. This is God. Write them down. Cling to these moments like a child clings to his mother. Why write down these consolations and good resolutions? Because consolation doesn't last. The voice of the enemy wants you to forget and abandon your commitments to God.

If we are trying to be good, it is the voice of the bad spirit that tries to discourage us. He wants to take us from the good path. This temptation is the ordinary activity of the devil—to suggest to us things that are beneath our nature, low, selfish, and sinful. He will discourage us and tell us, "You aren't really making progress, prayer is a waste of time, God doesn't love you. God doesn't see you or care about you. You are way too busy today." He makes us feel inadequate, that holiness isn't important, and that for us it is impossible. The voice of the enemy tells us that things are worse than they are, and that other people are far holier than us. "Holiness is impossible for a sinner like you. Just quit."

The voice of evil tries to fill us with fear. When we feel far from God, when we feel like quitting, or when our soul is filled with an interior darkness, we call this a time of desolation. Be aware if you are in desolation. Consider being in desolation a diabolical attack. Notice that the devil doesn't appear in the form of a monster. When he attacks, you don't see a hideous beast. He is more subtle; he prefers to remain hidden like a serpent in the garden. His voice is often soft and made to sound a lot like yours. The bad spirit is a discourager, a whisperer, and a seducer. He plants seeds of doubt and fear and anxiety.

Consolation and desolation; this is true spiritual warfare. These are the movements we must discern. Know when you are under attack, and don't entertain these doubts or temptations. Evil thoughts are like an intruder trying to break into your home. They appeal to your intellect, and if they go to the intellect, they will impact the heart. The evil one knocks on the door, and if you open the door, he puts his foot in and now has entrance into your home. St. Ignatius says, when you are in temptation or desolation, do not listen. Fight back and do not make a change. Keep your convictions and resolutions you made when you had a sense of the presence of God. St. Ignatius is clear: We must fight back and not give in.

The Rosary is truly the greatest tool for spiritual warfare and the discernment of spirits. Who is it that brings desolation? The evil spirit. Mary has the power to crush the head of the serpent. She crushes desolation.

You want consolation. What is another name for the Holy Spirit? The Consoler. Mary is the spouse of the Holy Spirit. St. Maximilian Kolbe teaches us that when the Holy Spirit sees Mary in a soul by their virtue or by their calling upon her name, the Consoler flies there. Add to this the promises associated with invoking the Holy Name of Mary. St. Bernard of Clairvaux teaches us that never was it known that anybody who called upon her was left unaided. You feel like you are drowning, your soul is dark, your eyes are filled with tears? Call upon the name of Mary. She will never fail. To the devil she is as terrible as an army in battle array.

St. Ignatius recommends that when we are in desolation, we should look back at the time of consolation and know that peace will return. When we are in consolation, hoard it like food for the winter. Know that desolation is imminent, like the changing of the season, so we need to prepare ourselves. The spiritual life is a series of cycles.

God allows the cycle of consolation and desolation for our growth and to honor our free will, but be assured Jesus and Mary are always close.

When we are in consolation, it is wise to write down our resolutions. Make them visible to our eyes. Pray with them; discern them, so that when the enemy returns, we can see the anointed message and be strengthened. Especially when praying in the presence of the Blessed Sacrament, bring a pen and paper. This is a most fertile place for discernment. Consult with Jesus and Mary about everything.

The Rosary truly is a fountain of inspiration and consolation. Often people will confuse inspirations they receive in prayer. "Every time I go to pray, these ideas pop into my mind." If asked to elaborate, they might say something like, "When I begin to pray the Rosary, all of a sudden it comes to mind that I promised to cook dinner for a family, that I have to go to the store to buy detergent, that I need to get my oil changed … Is this bad?"

No. These are not distractions! Get a pen and make a list. When you are praying the Rosary, the Spirit of God is being stirred up and putting on your heart all the things that God wants you to do. Write down these things, even if they seem insignificant or mundane. Your prayer will lead to an ordered and organized life. The Holy Spirit is trying to help you. These convictions that come in prayer, write them down too. Use the Rosary as your means of conversation with Jesus and Mary. Pray the Rosary with a still and listening disposition, and linger in the mystery for a moment so that God may speak to you.

"Union with the Immaculata, to be an instrument in her immaculate Hands: here is the secret which guarantees success," says St. Maximilian Kolbe.[70] Consult with Jesus and Mary about everything, especially about your prayer life. In your Rosary, ask the question, "Mary, how many Rosaries do you want me to pray? How often should I go to Confession? Do you want me to go to daily Mass?" When it is God that puts the answer in your heart, when He says, "Pray the Rosary every day," He gives you the grace to accomplish it—but you must ask.

Countless times I have been at an impasse and didn't know what direction to take in life, but I asked the Blessed Mother and then prayed a decade of the Rosary. She has never failed. I don't get divine revelations. I haven't had any visions. But in the depth of my soul, I am convicted of what I need to do. If I have failed, it is because of me, but she never fails. This is the secret to Marian devotion. When you pray and ask Mary for God's will, this is the surest, safest way to know. And when you know, write it down, because the consolation doesn't last.

Think of Peter, James, and John at the Transfiguration. They were so amazed that they wanted to put up a tent and remain in the presence of Jesus' transfigured glory. That time of elation passes. God allows us to be tested, and then the devil comes to sow doubt.

Let's say you have been reading this book, and during the section on mental prayer you were filled with zeal and conviction. "I must use mental prayer." This conviction, this movement to do good was the "voice" of God. However, later, when it was time to pray the Rosary, you heard a different voice. "You are tired. Just pray the Rosary like you have always done it, and you can try mental prayer later."

My brothers and sisters, that is a subtle attack, but the devil is a master strategist. He knows that if we pray with mental prayer, and it becomes a habit, he has lost. Mental prayer won't actually make us more tired. Mental prayer revives our drooping power and is the ordinary means for removing weariness from the soul. Praying the Rosary with mental prayer draws down extraordinary grace and renews us and stirs up the power of God in us. The enemy uses the path of least resistance and makes a small suggestion. Our response should be to do the opposite of his suggestion. When darkness enters your soul, when the spirit of confusion invades your mind, turn to mental prayer. Turn to the Rosary.

In your meditation, the light of Christ will shine out in the darkness. Our Lady will see to it that you have some direction. Remember, St. Ignatius of Loyola insists that we never make a change in times of desolation. Keep the resolutions you made while in the presence of God. Follow the plan. If God wants to change the plan, wait until you are in a time of consolation. St. Ignatius goes one step further, saying that if you are in desolation, if you are under attack, fight back with more than originally planned. Pray even better. The devil is a coward when he is met with a firm conviction and confidence in God. The Rosary is the perfect weapon with which to fight back, because it requires constancy and repetition.

To say you are going to pray the Rosary day in and day out, rain or shine, gets you in the habit of doing the hard thing when you aren't feeling like it. This is emotional and spiritual maturity. The consistency is also helpful when God asks us to do something challenging; coming back to Him multiple times a day makes it difficult to avoid our resolutions. Knowing that we will face Jesus and Mary again, we have to carry out their requests.

It will happen sometimes that you have prayed and prayed about a question, and you still don't know what to do. A deadline is fast approaching, and you have no light from on high. In that case, trust that because you have asked Mary's input and she gave no insight, she is asking you to look at the data and make the most reasonable choice. In this case trust your conscience. In the last analysis of our lives, did we follow our best judgment? If so, we have chosen well. The *Catechism* instructs us:

> Deep within his conscience man discovers a law which he has not laid upon himself but which he must obey. Its voice, ever calling him to love and to do what is good and to avoid evil, sounds in his heart at the right moment.... For man has in his heart a law inscribed by God.... His conscience is man's most secret core and his sanctuary. There he is alone with God whose voice echoes in his depths.[71]

If we want to do God's will, and we have done everything in our power to know it and carry it out, we should make the best choice and trust that God will bring good out of all of our best efforts. Even if in the end we are wrong, because we earnestly tried to do God's will and went with Mary, she will see to it that the greatest good comes from even our mistakes.

The more you intentionally seek after God's will, the more you will become docile to His promptings. These principles and this newfound openness to the Holy Spirit are essential as we grow in holiness. As you make progress in the spiritual life, the tactics of the devil do change, but I promise you will not be conquered if in humility you cling to Mary.

When the time comes that the devil knows that he can't directly trap you in mortal sin, his approach will become more subtle, and he will tempt you with lesser goods. If he can't have you with him in Hell, at the very least he can try and limit the good you do and limit your sanctity. But, if you consult with Mary and cling to the Holy Rosary, she will guide you through all phases of the spiritual life, and you will arrive at the height of sanctity.

> *If you say the Holy Rosary every day, with a*
> *spirit of faith and love, Our Lady will make sure*
> *she leads you very far along her Son's path.*
>
> — St. Josemaría Escrivá[72]

DIABOLICAL OBSESSION, OPPRESSION, AND FREEDOM

This is a very serious and very sensitive topic. If you are experiencing what I am about to describe, this is a circumstance where I strongly recommend praying all the mysteries of the Rosary (four sets) every day.

Temptations come as whispers from the enemy for every man, woman, and child, but the devil does also act in extraordinary ways. I am not talking about Hollywood-type events, because even in his extraordinary activity, he wishes to remain hidden. The extraordinary activity of the devil can be broken down into two categories: an infestation of a location or a person.

I want to address two types of personal infestation. People use different terms, but we are going to use the terms diabolical *obsession* and diabolical *oppression*. This topic isn't often discussed, but these phenomena are far more common than people realize.

Diabolical obsession is what it sounds like. The devil tempts you in an extreme way, and you are harassed with obsessive thoughts about a particular vice. The most common diabolical obsession involves demons of lust, but it can also be fear, sadness, and anxiety. The devil is waging a war on our thoughts to get us to sin or to keep us from thriving. Often when a person is in an addictive cycle of sin and they can't seem to break it, there is more than just chemical addictions at play, and demons are exerting extra pressure on the victim.

For our example, we will discuss combating demons of lust, but these principles apply to any obsession or diabolical slavery. In 1917, Our Lady warned little Jacinta of Fatima that more souls go to Hell because of sins of the flesh than for any other vice. I imagine that this is still true.

A normal temptation to lust comes as a simple passing sexual thought, a suggestion to do an evil act. A normal temptation can easily be combated by cultivating the virtue of purity, redirecting your thoughts, or offering a quick prayer. When a person is experiencing a diabolical obsession of lust, it is an extreme temptation, an enveloping cloud of darkness in the mind. It feels almost as if it is impossible to resist, as if a person's brain is flooded with sexual perversions and constant thoughts to commit sin. It can feel like a force is on your shoulders weighing on you. The intellect becomes obsessed with thoughts of perversion and impurity. A good analogy is to imagine you are trying to drive a car down the highway. An outside force grabs the wheel and is trying to slam your car into oncoming traffic, and you are fighting with every fiber of your being not to let that happen. You have the will to resist, but if you let down your guard for even a moment, you will crash. This type of temptation can only be overcome with divine grace and great effort. As Bishop Hugh Doyle says, "No one can live continually in sin and continue to say the Rosary: either they will give up sin or they will give up the Rosary."

If you commit to pray all the mysteries of the Rosary every day, there is no vice that cannot be overcome. Our Lady of the Rosary has already broken the chains of bondage for countless souls. She has crushed the demons you wrestle with countless times. But you have to trade slavery to the devil for a holy "slavery" to Mary. When the person commits to praying four sets of mysteries a day, they are always liberated.

One of the promises that Mary made to Bl. Alan for those who prayed the full Rosary is that it would "destroy vice"! These four Rosaries will be the foundation for you to become a saint, but more than just four Rosaries are necessary to overcome your demons. What the four Rosaries will do is reduce the severity of the diabolical temptation, sometimes down to an ordinary temptation. Now you have a fighting chance, but you still need to develop virtue. You will need to do some fasting and mortification of your appetites, go to Confession regularly, and receive Jesus in the Eucharist and visit Him. You will probably also need to moderate your screen time. Many things need to be done, but the foundation is the Rosary. This will provide the grace for all the other changes, and it will beat back the devil. First, you will go a week without falling, then a month, then two months, and then it will be years. With the Rosary, you will begin to have glimpses of Heaven on earth. If you are stuck in a cycle of sin, commit to trying it for nine days as a starting point. You will not regret it.

Diabolical oppression is when an evil spirit impacts us physically or exacerbates a preexisting condition. Earlier I mentioned anxiety, fear, and depression. Let me be clear: I am not saying that all mental or emotional disturbances are diabolical. The devil is not behind every rock, every inconvenience, illness, or hardship. It is true, however, that evil spirits can sometimes impact our health and exacerbate preexisting conditions. It is also true that demons can cause lethargy, anxiety, brain fog, illness, depression, suicidal thoughts, and insomnia.

Not every discomfort is diabolical, and God does answer prayers and can heal us, both body and soul. It's also important to consult medical professionals, but use spiritual common sense. If you are putting on a retreat and every time you go to prepare for the retreat, you are hit with brain fog and drowsiness, or if every time you take out your Rosary you get a panic attack or a migraine, something else might be at play.

I have heard many testimonies of people who have taken on the full Rosary solely for the purpose of growing in holiness, and then they are surprised that suddenly a long-term illness or mental disorder stops. "After I started praying the four Rosaries my anxiety stopped." "When I started praying the entire Rosary, I no longer had insomnia." This isn't every case, but it does happen.

Even if you pray the entire Rosary every day, you may still suffer bouts of a particular diabolical obsession/oppression. St. John Vianney prayed the entire Rosary every day, and the devil would come and harass him. It was a sign; he was doing great things, and the devil was about to lose major ground. Stay close to Mary. The devil takes a beating when you persevere in your Rosary. He will retreat. Nothing is outside the control of God. Even if you are experiencing some torment, God is in control. He is allowing it. Trust in Him. Growing in the interior life is often a painful experience, but with the Rosary, suffer well and with courage. Our Lady is with you.

Finally, a serious warning. If you have a diabolical obsession or oppression and you begin praying the full Rosary, your circumstance may suddenly and significantly worsen. Notice the connection. Do not quit. That sudden spike in your symptoms in response to prayer is an indication that the demon is trying to shake you from this habit. This can be a sign that the Rosary was effective and the devil was trying to scare you away. I have seen situations where a person tries to pray the Rosary for the first time, and they are physically pinned down! If that happens, cry out to Mary. Just saying the name of Mary in situations like this will send the evil spirit packing! Be consoled, the devil only acts out like that when he is desperate and knows he is going to lose you. Keep going!

I am sorry if this section scared or bothered you, but this is real. So many people are struggling in a hidden bondage. Our Lady has come to set the captives free. The children of Mary have nothing to fear. Mary is with us. Pray the Rosary and sleep peacefully.

Our Lady of the Rosary, Our Lady of Victory, pray for us!

THE PRIEST, THE ROSARY, AND SPIRITUAL WARFARE

If the priest is a saint, the people will be fervent; if the priest is fervent, the people will be pious; if the priest is pious, the people will at least be decent. But if the priest is only decent, the people will be godless.

— Dom Jean-Baptiste Chautard, O.C.S.O.[73]

A priest goes to Heaven or a priest goes to Hell with a thousand people behind him.

— St. John Vianney[74]

The most powerful person on earth is a Catholic priest. The devil hates priests more than he hates any other individuals. The devil hates the family because the family is an image of the Trinity, but the priest literally acts in the Person of Christ. The Catholic priest has the power to make Jesus Christ present on our altars and the power to bring countless souls dead in sin back to life. Just as the father is the head of the family, the Catholic priest is the spiritual head of all the families in his parish boundaries. If the father of a family must spend himself on his knees, praying for his family and tirelessly making sacrifices, how much more the father that all the other fathers call "Father"!

A priest must be under Mary's mantle and protection. The devil is more cunning than we can imagine, and will watch and wait years for a strategic attack. He will allow a priest to build up a following and reach a place of prominence, just so that his fall will damage as many people as possible. We have seen it so many times. Priests must pray the Rosary. Our Lady protects her children.

This is a very difficult time to be a priest. Priests are often scattered with no community, with nobody to check on them or keep them accountable, and the devil can set innumerable traps. A priest can receive a single, unsubstantiated accusation and have his reputation ruined. And yet even in these difficult times, God is calling men to say yes to the priesthood and yes to becoming a saint. All the promises of the Rosary apply especially to priests.

The devil whispers, "You already prayed the Divine Office. This is the liturgy of the Church. This is required. This is sufficient." I will be the first to say that the Liturgy of the Hours is beautiful, rich, and powerful. It is the prayer of the entire Church, and it is the minimum for a priest to pray. If he doesn't do this bare minimum, he is in mortal sin. And yet, the minimum has resulted in mediocrity, scandal, and a dying Church in many places.

Our Lady can work wonders through a priest willing to totally surrender himself to her. A holy priest is like the leader of an army. The devil told St. John Vianney that if there were only three priests like him on this earth, the kingdom of Hell would be destroyed. To be a faithful priest is to be another Christ. To be another Christ, it is essential to love Mary and to relate to her from the heart.

When a priest is intensely Marian and prays the Rosary, he will experience fruitfulness and growth in ministry. Every priest canonized since the Reformation has prayed the Liturgy of the Hours *and* the Rosary. I have yet to find a canonized priest who didn't pray the Rosary, including Popes St. John XXIII, St. Paul VI, and St. John Paul II. It was the Rosary that helped to make these men holy. Priests must be men of prayer; priests must strive to be saints.

My day must be one long prayer; prayer is the breath of life.
I propose to recite all fifteen decades of the Rosary every
day, if possible in the chapel before the Blessed Sacrament.
— St. John XXIII[75]

Seven Reasons Priests Should Pray the Rosary

The Rosary was designed by the Mother of God to help her children become saints. Here are seven reasons her sons — especially priests and other clergy — should pray the Rosary every day.

1. Every man needs the emotional support of a woman.

Every man was made naturally for the companionship of a woman, just as every woman was made for the companionship of a man. Because a priest is a celibate man, this emotional support must come from the Blessed Mother. She is a real woman. She is alive. She speaks. She makes her presence felt. The priest as an image of Christ is designed for emotional intimacy with Mary. She will counsel him, comfort him, and advise him. She will strengthen him and love him. In the daily recitation of the Rosary, we develop a relationship with Mary that is real. In many places the priest lives alone, with no brother priests to keep him accountable. In the constant return to Our Lady every day, she does communicate to the priest habits he needs to correct.

2. *By spending real time with Mary and Jesus in the Rosary, the Hearts of Jesus and Mary become the priest's heart.*

What they love, the priest begins to love. Imagine yourself daily in prayer with Mary, standing at the foot of the Cross, watching Our Blessed Lord suffer. Their Sacred and Immaculate Hearts burn with love for souls, setting our hearts on fire. Zeal for souls is contagious; in ministry, the passion for souls comes out in preaching and in actions. It is so easy for a layperson to notice when a priest has a love for souls, just as we notice when a priest treats his vocation like a nine-to-five job. The difference is deep prayer.

3. *The priest that prays the Rosary is consistently pondering the sacrifice of Christ and is therefore generous with the mercy of God.*

If a priest acts like we have inconvenienced him to hear a Confession, this is a sign of a poor prayer life. There are many incredible parishes with generous Confession schedules, and in these places, you will find that the pastor is devoted to the Rosary. Think of all the priest-saints such as St. John Bosco, St. John Vianney, St. Alphonsus, St. Francis de Sales, St. Padre Pio, St. John Paul II, and Ven. Fulton Sheen. All these were men of the Rosary, and all these men loved to be in the confessional. Their greatest desire was to reconcile the people of God.

4. *When a priest spends his time in mental prayer with Christ, witnessing miracles and encountering the power* *of the Resurrection in the Gospels, it deeply impacts his eucharistic faith.*

The priest will begin to speak like it and act like it, and in his free time, he will go spend time with Jesus. He will begin to encourage his parishioners to have confidence in the Eucharist and push them to make holy hours of Adoration. He himself will organize public processions. His confidence in the power of the Eucharist and the power of what Christ can do is strengthened and renewed day after day with the Rosary. When the priest preaches on the Eucharist, his faith is imparted. He speaks about the Real Presence with conviction, and when the priest deeply believes it, the way he says it persuades all those who hear him.

5. *A priest is called to be the mediator between God and His people.*

After the Mass, the Rosary is the best prayer for begging God for grace for His people. Recall the life of St. John Vianney, the patron of parish priests. The church was empty when he was installed as pastor at Ars. It was the fervent, long prayer of the Holy Rosary on his knees before the Blessed Sacrament that obtained the grace of conversion for his town. Day after day and hour after hour, St. John Vianney would pray for the conversion of his people. Soon enough, all of France was traveling to Ars. This is the model for all parish priests.

6. *A priest is the guardian of the souls in his congregation, but they are Mary's children.*

When the priest becomes a true child of the Rosary, Mary, the refuge of sinners, will begin to communicate to the priest what she wants him to do. He won't hear words, but she will put it on his heart what he is to preach about and the specific points she wants him to make. If he obeys this prompting, something special then happens. The same Spirit that inspired the message also delivers it. The Holy Spirit inflames the priest with the charisms necessary to communicate the message. Pray the Rosary and Our Lady will put on your heart the message for your sermon. Pray the Rosary, and Our Lady will obtain for you the charisms necessary to succeed, because now it is no longer you figuring things out, but the Mother of God who is guiding you. She will convict you to say difficult things and do difficult things.

7. *Finally,* Nemo dat quod non habet*: You cannot give what you do not have.*

The people of God need to hear the Rosary preached. How can you preach a devotion you do not keep? You must know the Rosary from the depths of your soul, so that you can speak of it with passion and conviction, speaking of its power from experience. The people in the pews are in desperate need of this message, and they need to hear it often. You have the remedy for their problems.

In the confessional, you will meet many men and women addicted to pornography; you will encounter people whose families are in shambles. What prescription can you offer for such hopeless and desperate situations? From experience, the Rosary. This is Heaven's answer. You will see conversions and changes you couldn't have dreamed of. Our speech comes from the flow of the heart. You preach about what you love; love the Rosary.

St. John Paul II exhorted, "Recite the Rosary every day. I earnestly urge Pastors to pray the Rosary and to teach people in their Christian communities how to pray it."[76] If you pray the Rosary every day, you will become the priest God created you to be, the priest that you sacrificed your life to become. How do I know? Because Mary promised it. Because we have seen it happen in the life of every great priest that we know and love. Don't be mediocre. Become the saint God created you to be.

One place we can look for insights into spiritual combat is J. R. R. Tolkien's Middle-earth. The situation in many parishes is a lot like the condition of Rohan and Théoden King as described in the second book of the *Lord of the Rings* trilogy. Things are not going well, but the pastor has been slowly conditioned by the enemy to be comfortable. He has been lulled into a false sense of peace and complacency, when there is actually a war waging around him. The enemy ravages families and destroys lives. Those still standing look to their king for leadership, but they get nothing.

In *The Two Towers*, Gandalf and his company go to Rohan to warn Théoden of the war and destruction that is coming. They enter the Golden Hall only to find Théoden under the false illusions of Gríma Wormtongue. Gandalf, looking like a humble beggar, whispers a hymn to Lady Galadriel and then delivers Théoden King from his illusions, while simultaneously thrusting Gríma to the ground. Theoden stands. While the king is still regaining his strength, Gandalf invites him to come outside into the light.

> "Your fingers would remember their old strength better, if they grasped a sword," says Gandalf. Slowly Théoden stretched forth his hand. As his fingers took the hilt, it seemed to the watchers that firmness and strength returned to his thin arm. Suddenly he lifted the blade and swung it shimmering and whistling in the air. Then he gave a great cry. His voice rang clear as he chanted in the tongue of Rohan a call to arms.
>
> "Arise now, arise, Riders of Théoden!
> Dire deeds awake, dark is it eastward.
> Let horse be bridled, horn be sounded!
> Forth Eorlingas!"

The guards, thinking that they were summoned, sprang up the stair. They looked at their lord in amazement, and then as one man they drew their swords and laid them at his feet. "Command us!" they said.[77]

Priests, this is your reality. Just as the heroes of Middle-earth wielded their weapons against the forces of darkness, a priest, through the Rosary, wields a powerful spiritual weapon in his own battle. The people of God want a leader. Take up the Rosary as your weapon, and remember the strength of the Mother of God is in your hands.

Our Lady of Victory, pray for us.

> *When the Holy Spirit has revealed this secret*
> *[the Rosary] to a priest and director of souls, how*
> *blessed is that priest! … If such a priest really*
> *understands this secret, he will say the Rosary*
> *every day and will encourage others to say it.*
>
> — St. Louis de Montfort[78]

CHAPTER 6

The Benefits and Promises of the Rosary

AT THE VERY BEGINNING of this book, I recommended that, as you pray the Rosary, you discern prayerfully what God is asking you to do. Everybody is at a different place in their spiritual life, so filter out what is not relevant to you, and cling to the things that resonate.

For example, the fifteen promises outlined later in this chapter were given to Bl. Alan de la Roche and St. Dominic de Guzmán with the understanding that to "pray the Rosary" meant to pray all the mysteries (at that time, there were fifteen rather than twenty). You might not be there yet. That's okay. Please do not let that distract you. These promises still apply to you to some degree. Similarly, you might be called to pray more than a full Rosary—more than all twenty mysteries—every day. These promises apply to you to a greater degree.

Before exploring the fifteen promises, I want to share with you what I consider to be the five greatest benefits of praying the Rosary. These benefits are based on theology, lives of the saints, and my own observations from the testimonies of people I know who keep the Rosary as the foundation of their spiritual lives.

FIVE MAJOR BENEFITS OF THE ROSARY

In the preceding chapters, I have touched on several benefits of the Rosary, but here I'd like to take a moment to outline some of my favorites.

1) Mary will be your constant companion, and you will have peace in your soul. When we pray the Rosary well, using mental prayer, the very first act is to call to mind the presence of Mary and to enter with her into the mysteries of Jesus Christ. Just having Mary close to you calms the soul, but she does more than just put her arm around us. She helps us to encounter Jesus Christ. In this encounter with Jesus and Mary, God opens His Heart to us. He reveals His will to us. More than that, He doesn't just convict us of what needs to be done, but He also provides the grace and strength to do it. This knowing, understanding, and doing the will of God is essential for having peace of soul.

The greatest desire of the human heart is deep and abiding happiness, which can only be given by God. We will not have eternal happiness in this life, but He gives us glimpses of what we will experience in the next. When a conflict arises and turmoil hits, the person who faithfully returns to the Rosary has peace.

Are you anxious? Are you distressed? Then call upon Mary and don't stop calling upon her, because never was it known that anyone who called upon her was left unaided.

> *The Holy Rosary was given to the faithful in order that they might have spiritual peace and consolation more easily.*
>
> — Pope St. Pius V[79]

2) You will experience an increase of gifts of the Holy Spirit. The Church teaches that at Baptism we all receive specific charisms, gifts for building up the Church. Some are extravagant and some simple, but they are all necessary and work together in harmony for the salvation of souls. St. Paul enumerates these gifts in the New Testament (see 1 Cor. 12), and they are still relevant today. We grow in these gifts as we grow in holiness. All the charisms exist in Jesus Christ; by spending time with Him — especially as we encounter Him in the mysteries of the Rosary and in the Gospels — His gifts grow in us. Some of the most gifted evangelists and preachers, the most gifted healers and prophets, the most gifted confessors were all committed to Our Lady's Rosary.

The crises of faith so prevalent in the Church today are related to a lack of faith in the Holy Spirit and a lack of understanding of the lifelong effects of the sacrament of Confirmation. At the Last Supper, Jesus warned the apostles that He would have to leave them so that we could receive the Holy Spirit (John 14:16–19), having already told them that He had come to set the earth on fire and how He wished it was already blazing (Luke 12:49). Jesus also promised that the Spirit would lead us, pray in us, and work wonders for the building up of the Church. This promise continues to be fulfilled in the sacrament of Confirmation, as the *Catechism* explains: "It is evident from its celebration that the effect of the sacrament of Confirmation is the special outpouring of the Holy Spirit as once granted to the apostles on the day of Pentecost."[80] Yet, so many people today receive the sacrament of Confirmation but never really step into a life in the Spirit.

After Pentecost, the apostles were fired up with conviction and passion. Every Catholic is called to live this life in the Spirit, but so few have that passionate love for Jesus Christ or the powerful conviction that the Holy Spirit provides.

The secret to an increase in the power of the Holy Spirit is an increased devotion to Mary. Just as she prepared the apostles at Pentecost, today she prepares the Church to receive the outpouring of the Spirit. "When the Holy Spirit, her spouse, finds Mary in a soul, he hastens there and enters fully into it," St. Louis de Montfort says. "He gives himself generously to that soul according to the place it has given to his spouse. One of the main reasons why the Holy Spirit does not work striking wonders in souls is that he fails to find in them a sufficiently close union with his faithful and inseparable spouse."[81]

When faithfully praying the Rosary, we are in the presence of Mary, where the Holy Spirit can constantly work in us. By spending time with Mary in the Rosary, she molds us, prepares us, and disposes us to be open and docile to the Holy Spirit. We begin to resemble her and grow in the virtues of Christ. Because of this resemblance to Jesus and Mary, the Spirit works even more. The Holy Spirit loves the Angelic Salutation; the Body of Christ was formed in the womb of Mary by the power of the Holy Spirit then, and therefore it is Mary and the Holy Spirit who continue the work of forming the Body of Christ today.

We are a Supernatural Church, and the Holy Spirit is alive and wants to work in us, but we must be receptive to His will and His ways. The more a person is given over to the regular recitation of the Rosary, the more the Holy Spirit is active in his life. *Veni Sancte Spiritus. Veni per Mariam!* (Come, Holy Spirit. Come through Mary!)

3) Your faith in, and love for, the Eucharist will exponentially increase. Faith in the Holy Eucharist is a gift from God. To have the interior conviction that Jesus Christ is really, truly, and substantially present in the Eucharist is one of the greatest gifts a person can receive, and Mary obtains this gift for all of those that recite the Rosary faithfully. The three theological virtues of faith in God, hope in God, and love of God are all properly ordered toward Jesus in the Holy Eucharist.

Bl. Bartolo Longo said, "The Rosary in a gentle, subtle way leads one to the Eucharist. Those who approach Jesus in thought, yearn to approach him in reality."[82] This is what Our Lady wants most for her children. When you begin to pray the Rosary faithfully, you will find that the Mother of God has you in front of the Eucharist more and more. You will find yourself at Mass more than just Sundays and days of obligation, and you will seek Him out at other times in Adoration. As you pray the Rosary and contemplate the Second Person of the Holy Trinity, you will see in the Eucharist the One you love. The One who came to earth as a tiny infant has once more humbled Himself, to be with you in the humble disguise of the consecrated host.

In the Rosary we see Jesus working wonders, especially in the Luminous Mysteries. We remember how He turned water into wine at Cana; we see Him transfigured on Mount Tabor; we see these miracles, and our confidence in His power increases. Without fail, everybody who takes on the Rosary as a lifestyle isn't just Marian; they become Eucharist-centered. The same Christ who raised the dead waits for us in the tabernacle.

As you meditate on the Resurrection of Christ in Adoration, before the eucharistic presence of the resurrected Christ, your faith in the Mass will radically increase. The Mass will soon become the most valuable and central action of your life.

The greatest prayer and sacrifice for the salvation of souls is the Holy Sacrifice of the Mass. Let us dispose ourselves with the Rosary and plunge ourselves into the infinite graces of the Mass. And though the Mass is a far greater prayer than the Rosary, it is the Rosary that best disposes a soul to receive grace and to understand the Mass. The Rosary truly transforms your understanding of—and appreciation for—the Eucharist and all the other sacraments.

What meditating on the mysteries of the life of Christ does for our faith in the Eucharist, it also does for the sacraments of Baptism, Matrimony, Confirmation, and Holy Orders. In the

Luminous Mysteries in particular, we see Christ entering into these sacraments. For example, thinking about the miracle at Cana reminds us to pray for our own marriage and to seek to "do whatever He tells you" in our family life. Seeing Jesus filled with the Holy Spirit at His baptism reminds us of the power of our own Baptism, and our identity as children of God is renewed again. In the Glorious Mysteries, when we recall the descent of the Holy Spirit at Pentecost, we have a renewed sense of our Confirmation and appreciation of the Holy Spirit's movement in our hearts. Just as the Church, in her wisdom, puts the same feast before us year after year to stir up the graces of that event or remind us of the life of a particular saint, the Rosary places the institution of these sacraments before our eyes every day.

In addition, the more time you spend with Christ and His Mother and contemplate the graces of the sacraments, the more you grow to hate sin. As you pray the Rosary before the Blessed Sacrament and you see in mental prayer what your sin has done to Christ in the Scourging at the Pillar, you aren't just ashamed of sin; you detest it. You want to be as pure as possible. You want to confess frequently so that you can become more and more sinless. Those who commit mortal sin separate themselves from God, become enemies of God. And the only sure antidote for this is the sacrament of Reconciliation.

God doesn't reject us; rather, when we sin mortally, we reject God. Many people are then convinced by the devil to avoid Confession. They listen to the whisper. They think the priest will judge them, or they are convinced that their sin is greater than God's mercy. Our Lady of the Rosary crushes those lies and drowns out the voice of the evil one. Like a good mother when her child falls into the filth of sin, Mary picks us up and cleans us off.

4) Praying the Rosary saves countless souls! Our Lady of Fatima, by her persistent request of the Rosary and sacrifice, has made it clear that these are effective means to reach souls.

During every Rosary, we petition Jesus to save us and "especially those in most need of your mercy." Our Lady brilliantly added this petition specifically because she knew it would be efficacious. When we pray the Rosary for our own intentions, Mary uses those graces to help souls all over the world.

The Rosary is also extremely efficacious because it helps us successfully discern God's will and obtain the grace to do it. The sacrifice of our will for the will of God doesn't just bring us peace of soul and make us holy, but it also obtains countless graces for the conversion of poor sinners. The constant death of self to do the will of God is like a fountain of life for souls in need.

Jesus told St. Faustina that the conversion of every sinful soul demands sacrifice.[83] Those who die to themselves day in and day out by the recitation of the Rosary save many souls, but especially those of their family and friends. Why? A person gives himself to Mary in a profound way when he takes the Rosary as a rule of life, and with each Rosary comes a *Totus Tuus*: We give ourselves totally to Mary, and Mary gives herself totally to us. If we fight valiantly to obtain grace for Mary's loved ones, she fights for our loved ones. Mary's goal is to make us like Christ, and to be fully like Him, she helps us to become co-redeemers with Him. She trains us to take up our own crosses for the salvation of others. Hopeless cases, impossible dreams, sinners so far gone that most family members had counted them lost are brought back to the Faith because one person offered his life to Mary by means of the Rosary.

A friend of mine had a nineteen-year-old daughter who was morally a mess, into all the wrong things and making terrible decisions. The mother resolved that she would pray all the mysteries of the

Rosary every day for the rest of her life for the salvation of her daughter. Her daughter left home in the middle of the night and got into a tragic car accident. When the mom arrived at the hospital, her daughter had already passed away. This mother was utterly devastated, but she was resolved to keep her promise to pray the Rosary, even then. In the middle of deep prayer, she heard the Blessed Mother say clearly, "The Father has been merciful! She is with us!" Peace flooded her soul, and in the midst of her grief, she was consoled.

I tell you this to give you hope. Our Lady loves you. She loves your children and family members more than you do. If you have somebody in your family who looks lost, don't let looks deceive you. Fight for them. Our Lady never loses. This is why the devil fights so hard to get us to abandon our prayers: He knows that if we pray the Rosary, perhaps thousands of souls are on the line. Mary, grant us the grace to persevere in the Rosary.

> *Those who pray the rosary do more for the benefit*
> *of the whole human race than all the orators and*
> *deputies, more than all the organizers, secretaries and*
> *writers, more than all the capitalists even if they would*
> *make their entire wealth available to the Church.*
>
> — Servant of God Joseph Kentenich[84]

5) Praying the Rosary helps us to reach the heights of holiness. The most difficult lesson in the spiritual life is to embrace the cross. We must not just be resigned to God's will; we must love God's will.

Through the Rosary, Mary helps us persevere, consoling and mothering us. However, the cross may not be removed from us, and our lives will not automatically be made easier. Tragedy strikes. We lose people we love. Illness hits us. These moments cause us to cry out and ask, "God, why!? How can a good God allow this?"

In difficult moments like these, we look to Christ. He didn't take away suffering, but He entered into the depths of human misery so that death doesn't have the final say. He gives us meaning and hope in tragedy. He enters into the worst suffering and death so that when we do too, we can encounter the power of the Resurrection.

No child of Mary escapes the cross. However, she prepares us to walk our own way of the cross. Her Son's journey becomes our journey. Our Lady allows her children to be well disciplined and often it seems as if our crosses are tailor-made for us, to help form us and mold us. According to St. Louis de Montfort, Mary dips the cross in honey. She makes it bearable. In our suffering, she shows us her face and encourages us. Trust this. Everything that happens has been permitted by God. This is the great mystery of suffering: In death we find life. For those consecrated to Mary, this is the advice of one of the greatest Marian saints to ever walk the earth, St. Maximilian Kolbe: "Let yourself be led by the Immaculata: whatever does not depend on your will, surely she allows it for your greater good, even if it comes from the ill will of others."[85] And, "That which does not depend on your will is the sure will of the Immaculata; therefore, do not lose your peace of mind."[86]

When tragedy comes, if we have the habit of returning to Christ by meditation on the Sorrowful Mysteries of the Rosary, He Himself will teach us how to love God's will. It is our nature to rebel against the cross, but He trains us. We walk with Him on His Way of the Cross. We see how Christ clings to the Cross, how Christ loves this Cross, because His Cross is our salvation.

By the Cross, Jesus turns the weight of human misery into the glory of the Resurrection. And so, as we take up our crosses to follow Him, we understand that we must die to ourselves for the sake of the kingdom. This is the height of holiness. Mary trains us for this moment, bead after bead, mystery after mystery. Mary prepares us to accept everything with humility and confidence.

We have a powerful example of this in the witness of St. Maximilian Kolbe. He was running the largest monastery on earth, over seven hundred friars, all for the Immaculata. He had printing presses and radio stations in Poland and Japan, all for the Immaculata. He was taking over the world, all for the Immaculata. And yet when the Nazis came and shut him down, he didn't rebel. His response was, "Yes, Mary." When they carted him to Auschwitz, he didn't fight back. His response again was, "Yes, Mary." He saw in this the sure will of the Immaculata; there must be a bigger plan. He was subjected to the worst treatment and abuse, but again, St. Maximilian was convinced that God was allowing this, and if he trusted, great good would come out of it.

Then, when one man escaped his unit and ten men were going to die as a consequence, St. Maximilian saw in this moment an opportunity to be more like Christ. He traded his life for that of one of the condemned. He and the nine others were taken to the starvation bunker, which was the size of a closet. Ten men crammed in, naked, no light, no toilets, no running water. Hell on earth. At any other time, this would have been a place where curses, obscenities, and despair ruled. Yet St. Maximilian turned this situation into a chapel. He led the men in hymns of praise to God. He prayed the Rosary. He encouraged his fellow condemned.

Where did he get this strength? Who could keep his spirits alive? Mary. Where sin abounds, grace abounds all the more. In prayer he allowed himself to be fully transformed by Mary into another Christ. We can say of St. Maximilian what we say of

Christ: "No greater love has a man than to give his life for a friend." If you commit to be faithful to the Rosary, she will teach you to love God's will. She will obtain for you the graces to reach the heights of holiness and to become a saint. In times of darkness, cling to the Rosary.

> *The other day I can't tell you how bad I*
> *felt — there was a moment when I nearly refused*
> *to accept — deliberately I took the Rosary*
> *and very slowly without even meditating or*
> *thinking — I said it slowly and calmly — the*
> *moment passed — but the darkness is so dark,*
> *and the pain is so painful — but I accept whatever*
> *Jesus gives and I give whatever he takes.*
> — St. Teresa of Calcutta[87]

THE FIFTEEN PROMISES OF THE ROSARY

These fifteen promises of the Rosary come from the writings of Bl. Alan. They were given to him and to St. Dominic with the understanding that all the mysteries were being prayed. I will include a little explanation as well as a quote from the saints to help illuminate these promises.

1. *"Those who faithfully serve me by the recitation of the Rosary shall receive signal graces."*

Signal graces are serendipitous events that coincide with something we have been discerning in prayer. Let me be clear, we do not take every occurrence to be a sign from God. This is no way to live your life. Use the Rosary to discern the will of God in prayer; then, as God puts something on your heart, an undeniable act of Providence might occur that supports what you have already discerned.

For example, when I was presented with the idea of writing this book, I was extremely hesitant. I am not a good writer, but in prayer I could sense that Mary wanted this. Just after finishing a Rosary in discernment, my daughter brought me two chocolates. Inside the wrapper of the chocolates were little messages. Both said the same thing: "Don't be afraid to start a new chapter." I understood. Usually signal graces are smaller "coincidences," and they come after you have resolved to do something. The grace comes as a confirmation or sometimes just as a wink from God letting you know He sees you. You aren't alone.

> *The Holy Rosary, together with heartfelt prayers,*
> *will indicate when and how to act, because in*
> *those moments it is she who directs, in those*
> *moments it is she who erases any difficulty.*
>
> — St. Maximilian Kolbe[88]

2. *"I promise my special protection and the greatest graces to all those who shall recite the Rosary."*

Although praying the Rosary doesn't mean we are not going to suffer, Mary does offer special protections to her children. My favorite example is from the life of St. John Paul II. It was the feast of Our Lady of Fatima — May 13, 1981 — and he was shot by the Turkish assassin Mehmet Ali Ağca. The fact that his life was spared on this particular feast day is a clear indication of the providence of God.

Medical professionals considered it miraculous that his vital organs were not punctured. St. John Paul II said, "Although one finger pulled the trigger, another guided the bullets." St. John Paul II was not spared from suffering — he later embraced his

Parkinson's disease with grace and courage—this is an example of special protection.

> *As the history of the Church makes clear, this very*
> *fruitful way of praying is not only efficacious in*
> *warding off evils and preventing calamities, but it*
> *is also of great help in fostering Christian life.*
> —Pope St. Paul VI[89]

3. *"The Rosary shall be a powerful armor against Hell. It will destroy vice, decrease sin, and defeat heresies."*

This promise is the reason I promote the Rosary so fervently. The Rosary destroys vice and helps you overcome sin. Those who pray the Rosary go from being slaves to being free, eventually becoming witnesses who help to liberate others. Men and women battling addiction of every kind, from drugs to porn, have found freedom in the Rosary. With Mary's help and the graces of the Rosary, no one is too far gone.

> *The Rosary is the weapon that wins all the battles.*
> —St. Padre Pio[90]

4. *"The recitation of the Rosary will cause virtue and good works to flourish. It will obtain for souls the abundant mercy of God. It will withdraw the hearts of men from the love of the world and its vanities and will lift them to the desire of eternal things."*

The Rosary is a foundation for spiritual growth. It is a fountain of grace that strengthens us to do other practical things like fasting, self-discipline, leaving unhealthy friend groups, and so forth. All these things are needed to overcome sinful habits. Is the Rosary all you need? No, but there is a reason that at Fatima, Mary, month after month, kept repeating the Rosary. Once the Rosary takes root in a person's soul, the other aspects of the spiritual life come more naturally. The Rosary is like a tree; its fruits are a rich sacramental life, holiness, charismatic gifts, devotion to the angels, spiritual reading, mortification, and so much more.

> *In places, families, and nations in which*
> *the Rosary of Mary retains its ancient*
> *honor, the loss of faith through ignorance*
> *and vicious error need not be feared.*
> — Pope Leo XIII[91]

5. ***"The soul that recommends itself to me by the recitation of the Rosary shall not perish."***

Anybody who cries out to Mary by praying the Rosary will not suffer eternal fire. St. Louis de Montfort goes further:

> If you say the Rosary faithfully until death, I do assure you that, in spite of the gravity of your sins "you shall receive a never fading crown of glory." Even if you are on the brink of damnation, even if you have one foot in Hell, even if you have sold your soul to the devil, and even if you are a heretic … sooner or later you will be converted and will amend your life and save your soul.[92]

6. ***"Those who recite my Rosary devoutly, applying themselves to the consideration of its sacred mysteries, shall never be conquered by misfortune. In His justice,***

God will not chastise them; nor shall they perish by an unprovided death."

At Fatima, Our Lady said that God allows wars as a punishment for sin. God gives humans free will and allows us to suffer the consequences of our actions. She also particularly warned that if people didn't pray the Rosary and better themselves, an even greater war was going to break out. In doing so, she identified the very sign that would precede World War II.

Two groups should have died during the atomic blasts of World War II but did not. In Hiroshima, very close to ground zero, there was a community of Jesuits who had the habit of daily Mass, Adoration of the Blessed Sacrament, and the Rosary. The atomic bomb destroyed everything around them and countless people died, but these Jesuits suffered only minor scrapes and bruises and no radiation poisoning. When questioned about how they survived, they said: "We are living the message of Fatima."

A second group, conventual friars founded by St. Maximilian Kolbe in Nagasaki, had built their friary on the side of a mountain, which was contrary to conventional Japanese wisdom. St. Maximilian said that Mary made it clear to him in prayer the precise location where the friary was to be built. A few years later, when the bomb was dropped in Nagasaki, the community was unharmed.

The Holy Rosary, according to Lucia of Fatima,
is so powerful that it can solve any problem,
material or spiritual, national or international.
— Bl. Gabriele Allegra[93]

7. *"Those who have a true devotion to the Rosary shall not die without the sacraments of the Church."*

The hour of death is one of the most important moments of your life. Saints have said that the demons attack the soul like flies to dung, tempting the soul to despair and to reject God. Death is scary, and many people have terrible agonies just before they die.

When you pray the Rosary daily, imagine the Hail Marys that will come flooding upon you at the hour of death and the graces hitting you all at once. No wonder so many of the great Marian saints, at the hour of their death, sit up in bed and see the radiant face of their Mother welcoming them to Paradise. St. Dominic Savio is the patron saint of boys. He died an early death, but some years later he appeared to his teacher and mentor, St. John Bosco, to tell him about death: "What comforted me most at the point of death was the assistance of the powerful and loving Mother of God."[94]

8. *"Those who faithfully recite the Rosary shall have, during their life and at their death, the light of God and the plenitude of His graces. At the moment of death, they shall participate in the merits of the saints in Paradise."*

Those who recite the Rosary have the light of God. When praying the Rosary, many of us begin to find incredible insights concerning Sacred Scripture, which is the result of the Holy Spirit working and God illuminating the intellect.

St. Thomas Aquinas, who possessed great intellect, said that he learned more from prayer than from books. I would rather hear a homily from a man of deep prayer than a man of deep learning; one speaks to the head, which is good, but the other speaks to the heart, and that is better. All the greatest saints were made saints by the intercession of the Mother of God.

From Mary, St. Thomas Aquinas sought
celestial wisdom daily with the Holy Rosary.
— Bl. James Alberione[95]

9. *"I shall deliver from Purgatory those who have been devoted to the Rosary."*

Purgatory is a place of purification for venial sins and imperfections. Purgatory, although painful, is a place of God's mercy. For children of the Rosary, Our Lady works all our lives to prepare us for the hour of death. She pours out graces for our commitment to her, and the constant self-denial and embrace of the will of God act as expiation and removal of the temporal punishment due to sin. If you pray the Rosary and respond to the graces God gives you, Mary will certainly deliver you from Purgatory.

St. Alphonsus Liguori in *The Glories of Mary* records the testimony of countless saints, telling how the Virgin Mary brings relief to the souls in Purgatory. In the diary of St. Faustina Kowalska, she describes the fires of Purgatory and how the Virgin Mary comes to their aid.

> I was in a misty place full of fire in which there was a great crowd of suffering souls. They were praying fervently, but to no avail, for themselves; only we can come to their aid.... I asked these souls what their greatest suffering was. They answered me in one voice that their greatest torment was longing for God. I saw Our Lady visiting the souls in Purgatory. The souls call her "The Star of the Sea." She brings them refreshment.[96]

Offer the Rosary for the souls in Purgatory. It is a great act of mercy to pray for them. These souls are so thankful for the relief you bring them that you will be assured of their prayers and assistance in return. Besides the Mass, there is no greater relief you can offer a soul in Purgatory than the praying of the Rosary. If a person was outside dying of thirst, would you not give them a glass of water? Include the poor souls in your prayers.

> *If we wish to be of material assistance to the souls in Purgatory,*
> *we must always recommend them in our prayers to the Blessed*
> *Virgin Mary, and especially offer the holy Rosary for them.*
>
> — St. Alphonsus Liguori[97]

10. *"The faithful children of the Rosary shall merit a high degree of glory in Heaven."*

In the eternal beatitude of Heaven, the soul experiences the greatest ecstasy. Every soul is filled to the brim, but not all souls are equal in Heaven. Just as a small water bottle and a large barrel can be totally full, yet the barrel is capable of carrying more, so it is with souls.

St. Louis de Montfort tells a story of a Carmelite nun who, after her death, returned to her sister in a vision. She mentioned that Heaven was incredible, but that if she could return to earth, she would be willing to suffer the worst torment for a thousand years just to receive the glory of having said one more Hail Mary. Our Lady promises that if you are faithful to her Rosary, she has a spot for you very close to her.

> *The greatest saints, those richest in grace and virtue,*
> *will be the most assiduous in praying to the most*
> *Blessed Virgin, looking up to her as the perfect model*
> *to imitate and as a powerful helper to assist them.*
>
> — St. Louis de Montfort[98]

11. *"By the recitation of the Rosary, you shall obtain all that you ask of me."*

Anytime God grants a petition, we call that a grace. Yet because He is good, God does not grant petitions that will not benefit us for salvation. If you are praying the Rosary for a Mercedes Benz, unless somehow that specific car is going to help you become a saint, I wouldn't count on it. What Mary is promising is that you will receive all that you need, and she is so good, she often gives far more than you could ever have desired. Perhaps you don't need a luxury car, but you really just need a ride to get to work. Our Lady will answer that need in some way.

Jesus said that if those who are sinful know how to give good gifts, how much more does the heavenly Father (see Matt. 7:11–12). The same applies to His Mother. St. John Bosco said, "Entrust yourself to Jesus in the Blessed Sacrament and to Mary Help of Christians, and you will see miracles." Trust her to provide for your needs. Pray the Rosary faithfully, and you will see the hand of a loving mother making a way.

> *No one has ever had recourse to her in vain.*
> *Entrust all your matters to Her and She shall*
> *deign to take care of them. In Her loving,*
> *immaculate hands, victory is certain.*
> — St. Maximilian Kolbe[99]

12. *"Those who promote the Holy Rosary shall be aided by me in their necessities."*

This promise is so important. Burn this saying into your mind; it cannot be overstated: Mary is not outdone in generosity. If we go out of our way to support her causes, she will support us in ours.

She is more generous than we are. If we strive to save her children, she will save our children.

The greatest act of charity you can show your neighbor is to help them save their soul. By promoting the Rosary, you don't just help them to find salvation, you help them to have the most meaningful life possible. Our Lady blesses our efforts when we promote the Rosary. St. Louis de Montfort said that a person does more good with a single lesson on the Rosary than with years of teaching on other topics. The Rosary changes our habits, and habits change our lives.

> *Our Lady blesses not only those who preach*
> *her Rosary, but she highly rewards all those*
> *who get others to say it by their example.*
>
> — St. Louis de Montfort[100]

13. *"I have obtained from my Divine Son that all the advocates of the Rosary shall have for intercessors the entire celestial court during their life and at the hour of their death."*

The saints are alive. All the saints that you have a devotion to — you didn't choose them; they chose you! Foster a relationship with these saints because Heaven has chosen them as your special friends. For those who pray the Rosary, every saint in Heaven is on your team, cheering you forward.

When I unite my mental prayer with my favorite saints, I often sense that they are urging me to keep going. The saints are with you now, and they will be waiting for you at the hour of your death to receive you in a great celebration in Heaven.

*The greater the charity of the Saints in their heavenly
home, the more they intercede for those who are
still on their journey and the more they can help
them by their prayers; the more they are united
with God, the more effective those prayers are.*

— St. Thomas Aquinas[101]

*Every saint belongs to the court of
the Queen of All Saints.*

— St. John Eudes[102]

14. *"All who recite the Rosary are my beloved children and the brothers and sisters of my only Son, Jesus Christ."*

This is the secret to sanctity: Love Mary as much as possible. The more you love her, the more you resemble her Son, Jesus Christ. If you took the love of every woman who ever lived and put it into one mother, that wouldn't equal the love Mary has for you.

*Love Mary! She is loveable, faithful, constant. She will never let
herself be outdone in love, but will ever remain supreme. If you
are in danger, she will hasten to free you. If you are troubled,
she will console you. If you are sick, she will bring you relief. If
you are in need, she will help you. She does not look to see what
kind of person you have been. She simply comes to a heart that
wants to love her. She comes quickly and opens her merciful
heart to you, embraces you and consoles and serves you. She
will even be at hand to accompany you on the trip to eternity.*

— St. Gabriel of the Sorrowful Mother[103]

15. *"Devotion to the Rosary is a great sign of predestination."*

What more can we ask for? The fact that you are faithful to your Rosary is the greatest sign that you will be in Heaven for eternity. When you surrender your life fully to Mary through the Rosary, she takes care of everything. She fights for your salvation, and she doesn't lose. According to St. Alphonsus in *The Glories of Mary*, "It has never happened and never will happen that a humble and devoted servant of Mary will be eternally damned."[104]

CONCLUSION

The number of effects and benefits of praying the Rosary as often as possible is far too great to list. In his book *The Secret of the Rosary*, St. Louis de Montfort also includes these benefits to those who pray the Rosary:

✠ Sinners are forgiven.

✠ Thirsty souls are refreshed.

✠ Those who weep find happiness.

✠ Those who are tempted find peace.

✠ The poor find help.

✠ The religious are reformed.

✠ The ignorant are instructed.

As long as there are souls on earth praying the Rosary, the list of benefits will continue to grow. Let us echo the words of St. Bernard, *"De Maria, numquam satis"*: Of Mary, we can never say enough.

Our Lady of the Rosary, pray for us!

CHAPTER 7

Rosary Success: Important Tips and Essential Advice

The Power of the Rosary is beyond description.
—Ven. Fulton Sheen[105]

Although convinced that the Rosary is powerful, many people still struggle to make it a regular part of the day. The devil will throw every excuse at you: "Later. Tomorrow. You're too tired. You're not good at this." In this chapter, we will examine strategies that have helped many to persevere. With God's grace, the Rosary won't be just another good intention but rather an unshakable habit that changes every aspect of your life. I am going to give you essential advice that could change the course of your family, for eternity.

Five Important Tips

1. Always carry a rosary with you. Carrying a rosary is the most practical sign of your intention to keep your devotion to the Rosary. Yes, theoretically you can pray the Rosary using your fingers, but from experience, this usually doesn't happen long-term. Rosary bracelets are good, and many people use them, but I still really encourage you to carry a five-decade rosary. Having a full rosary on your person is a powerful reminder of the presence of Mary.

When a stressful situation arises or an accident happens, the rosary in your hand acts as a reminder, "No. I am not at the mercy of this situation." Simply holding the rosary in your hand brings grace and comfort. Don't be afraid to carry your "weapon." In such a secular culture, to carry the rosary openly on a bus or in a train can be just what a desperate person needs to see. Pope Innocent XI decreed that you receive a partial indulgence for carrying the rosary as a sign of devotion.

Get a nice durable rosary; it can be emotionally discouraging when you reach in your pocket to pull out your rosary, and it is in two pieces. A good, strong rosary can make a special gift for a family member. Many people spend a lot of money on phones that they always carry with them, but the rosary is an item that we really shouldn't be ashamed to spend money on. We also use it to communicate and should always carry it with us.

> *In the moments when fever, agony, and pain make*
> *it hard to pray, the suggestion that comes from*
> *merely holding the rosary ... is tremendous.*
> —Ven. Fulton Sheen[106]

2. Have a special intention. Start with a novena. You will do any "what," if you have a good "why." Remember your "why." What intention can you formulate that is so important to you that it can act as a motivation to pray, even when you don't want to? Ideally, we pray because we love God and want to grow in holiness, but for most of us, we need a little more motivation. In time, God will purify our intentions, but for now pick a major "why." Choose something so important that it will keep you going long after you want to quit.

A novena is a powerful way to establish the importance of a particular intention. To make a novena, select a certain number of days that you will try and complete. This is especially helpful for people who have never prayed the Rosary before, or those who are trying to pray multiple Rosaries for the first time. Some people make a nine-day novena; some will commit to it during Lent or Advent. Another popular novena is the 54-Day Novena.

Again, this novena can be of a single Rosary or multiple, depending on your situation. The point of this isn't that you quit after nine or fifty-four days, but that you set a goal long enough to make it a habit. You see that it is actually doable and your life is better because of it.

3. Pray the introductory prayers just once a day. Of all the tips of the Rosary, this one often makes the biggest difference for people. The Rosary was originally intended to be one long prayer but split up through the day. If you are praying multiple Rosaries, you don't need to repeat the introductory prayers each time. Once you pray the Apostles' Creed at the start of the day, it isn't necessary to pray it again later. Remember what makes the Rosary the Rosary: The Our Father, the Hail Mary, and most especially, the mysteries of the life of Christ. These are the essentials; where the power is. The other prayers are good, but if they are a stumbling block, don't let them keep you from praying a full Rosary.

4. Don't be too scrupulous. The devil throws everything he can at you to get you to quit this devotion. The most common attack is dryness and distraction, but just get it done. There is a common misconception that unless you *feel* warm and fuzzy, prayer isn't working. That is false. The spiritual life is often arduous, because it is a training in true love. When you don't "feel" it and pray (love) anyway, it is more meritorious.

The fruit of persevering in aridity is abundant. A friend of mine committed to praying the full Rosary for fifty-four days for his wife, who was really struggling in her faith. She was jobless, depressed, and hadn't been to Confession in over a year. He wasn't sure he could do it—four Rosaries sounded like a lot, and fifty-four days is a long time. He had a lot of bad days; many days he felt like he was just going through the motions, and his wife's situation seemed to be getting worse. He pushed forward, and on day fifty, his wife suddenly went to Confession. She came home a totally different woman. Now she is arguably more faithful than him! What if this good husband had quit on day twenty? He wasn't feeling anything, but he kept going. All of that desolation and his perseverance paid off. Feelings are nice, consolation is amazing, but we don't live there all the time.

Some people say that they start praying, and they forget what bead they are on and start all over. Don't start over. Keep going. Remember that the Rosary is both meditation and vocal prayer. The human mind cannot always do both well at the same time; one will struggle. If you start your meditation, some time has passed, and you look at your hands and they are on the ninth bead but you don't remember saying a single Hail Mary, my rule of thumb is: give it three Hail Marys and move on. Don't keep starting over. Some days you focus on the words more. Some days you are caught up to the heavens in mental prayer. Just get it done. Don't be too scrupulous, but absolutely do your best. Sometimes your best isn't very good, and that's fine.

5. Make a plan. The secret to success in the world and in the spiritual life is the same. You need to make a plan. When are you going to pray the Rosary? Think concretely. If your goal is to pray the Rosary once a day or four times a day, you need to be practical about when it is going to happen, or, sooner rather than later, it will stop happening. If you are trying to start praying four Rosaries a day, consider this recommended schedule: Wake up thirty minutes earlier than is necessary for you to get ready for your day, and pray your first Rosary. Praying immediately upon waking fills the entire day with grace and helps you to remain recollected during the day. Even if you are tired, Our Lady appreciates your efforts. I recommend kneeling or sitting straight up so you don't fall back asleep.

Pray your second Rosary on the way to work or school drop-off or while completing some morning chore. Pray your third Rosary on the way home at the end of the day. Pray your fourth Rosary with your family or before bed.

Some people love to go on Rosary walks; some can sneak away to a chapel. Figure out what schedule works for you. You'll note this recommended schedule doesn't necessarily impact family or free time. We can pray while we drive, do chores, or do other mindless tasks. "All the idle moments of one's life can be sanctified thanks to the Rosary," Ven. Fulton Sheen observed. "As we walk the streets, as we are driving an automobile.... While waiting to be served at a lunchroom, or waiting for a train, or in a store, or when a lecture lags—all these moments can be sanctified and made to serve inner peace."[107]

As a child, my grandmother had to do a breathing treatment first thing in the morning before going anywhere and again as the last thing before going to bed. Prayer is oxygen for the soul and is essential, and we make time for what is essential.

If we don't have a plan, the voice of the evil one will whisper, "Pray later." Next thing you know, it is past our bedtime, and we are lying in bed with the Rosary. For most of us, that means falling asleep halfway through.

> *You always leave the Rosary for later, and you end*
> *up not saying it at all because you are sleepy....*
> *The Holy Rosary is a powerful weapon. Use it with*
> *confidence and you'll be amazed at the results.*
>
> — St. Josemaria Escriva[108]

The Family Rosary

*It is the Rosary prayed by families that will keep
the lights of faith glowing in the days of darkness.*
— Ven. Patrick Peyton[109]

The single most important habit for a family is praying the family Rosary. The Rosary organizes and disposes souls to grow in all areas of the spiritual life. It is so beneficial that the devil puts up every obstacle to keep it from happening and works tirelessly to stop it once it has begun. In this section, we will look at different phases of family life to address the opportunities and obstacles that occur when implementing the family Rosary. Two important notes before we get into it.

First: *The family Rosary, if it is going to be effective and persevering, must start with and flow from your own personal commitment to the daily Rosary.* Your daily Rosary is going to supply the grace to successfully implement and sustain the family Rosary. The family Rosary is often difficult, dry, and full of distractions. That is okay. That doesn't mean it's bad or didn't work, but just be aware the temptation to quit will be constantly at the back of your mind; you know from whom that comes. The only way to persevere in this is through your own private prayer on behalf of the family.

You must be convinced that the Rosary is a fountain of life and protection for your family. The best way to safeguard the family Rosary is that at least one spouse must be praying the Rosary faithfully outside of the family Rosary. When everybody wants to quit, your commitment to the individual Rosary must come first and remain strong, and that is true at every stage of family life. It starts with you.

Second important note: *No two families are the same.* Praying the Rosary a certain way may work for one family, but that doesn't mean it will work for yours. Every situation has different dynamics. Some households are very fragile. You need to be sensitive to the temperaments of your family and graceful with each member—and also sensitive to other families that might do things a little differently. That being said, fighting for the family Rosary is worth it. Families can be totally transformed, but at least one person must be all in.

> *We exhort all Catholic Families to*
> *introduce the Rosary into their lives,*
> *and to encourage its propagation.*
> — St. Paul VI[110]

Young Couples

> *The family that prays together, stays together.*
> — Ven. Fr. Patrick Peyton[111]

The surest method of discerning your vocation is to be faithful to the Rosary. This is also true when you are discerning whom to marry. The Virgin Mary is an all-powerful mother, and she loves you more than your very own mother. She wants you to have the best spouse, even more than you desire it for yourself! She wants you to marry someone who will make you happy in this life, yes, but most importantly, she wants you to marry the person who will help you be happy in the next life. If you are faithful to her and entrust your relationship to her by praying the Rosary, she will be your sure guide and protection. Trust that she wants you to find the right spouse.

Remember, the goal of a spouse is to get his or her partner to Heaven! Then, to get the children to Heaven. How can a man fight for his spouse and children to get to Heaven if he himself constantly lives in mortal sin? How can a woman train her children in virtue and devotion if she doesn't keep a devotion and she lacks virtue? Make Jesus and Mary the center of your lives by praying the Rosary daily. When the Rosary is the heart of your heart, it will flow naturally into your relationships.

Make it clear during your courtship that you want to entrust your future to Mary. Make the Rosary a regular part of your relationship from the start. Our Lady uproots hidden vices and guards couples. Pray the Rosary together. Go on Rosary walks together. If time is limited, at the very least always pray a decade together. If you do this, Mary will guide and guard your relationship.

Impurity so often blinds us to the will of God. Our Lady is synonymous with chastity; pray the Rosary, and she will protect your purity. If you are meant for one another, she will make it evident. Always make your intentions clear from the beginning: "I want a holy family. I want a family that prays together and stays together." I know it is difficult to find a person who loves God, the Church, Mary, and the Rosary. This person is truly like a treasure buried in a field. Trust Mary. She will guard your heart and guide you to the right person.

> *If you recite the family Rosary, all united, you shall taste*
> *peace; you shall have in your homes a concord of souls.*
> —Ven. Pius XII[112]

Newlyweds

> *Starting on their wedding day, my parents knelt each*
> *evening before the hearth to say together the family*
> *Rosary, that God and Mary might protect and bless*
> *their home and fill it with the laughter of children.*
> —Ven. Patrick Peyton[113]

Consecrate your family to the Sorrowful and Immaculate Heart of Mary. Live this consecration by enshrining the daily family Rosary as one of the pillars of your marriage. It is so important to do this from the beginning, because the earlier a habit is established, the more chance it has to succeed. Remember that you must cultivate the habit of praying at least one Rosary on your own as a safeguard for the family Rosary.

The family Rosary is like a "tree planted beside the waters that stretches out its roots to the stream: It does not fear heat when it comes, its leaves stay green; In the year of drought it shows no distress, but still produces fruit" (Jer. 17:8).

Begin to think about what you want your family Rosary to look like as your family grows. Will you kneel before an image of Mary? Will you light a candle? What time will you pray? Decide now what will be your most cherished family tradition.

The family that recites the Rosary together reproduces
something of the atmosphere of the household of
Nazareth: its members place Jesus at the center.
— St. John Paul II[114]

Families with Young Children

From my earliest memories, I saw my
father with the Rosary beads in his hands
and my mother holding hers.
— Ven. Patrick Peyton[115]

For couples with young children, my heart honestly fills with joy thinking about how beautiful it is for a child to grow up thinking that the family Rosary is normal, thinking of the beautiful memories you will have ingrained into your mind of praying with your children. Hearing your son say the Hail Mary for the first time or telling your daughter the story of how Jesus died—so many beautiful moments will flow from teaching your children the Rosary.

Here are some practical tips. If you have the habit of praying the Rosary while you drive, when your children are very young begin to pray that car Rosary aloud. This habit will make praying the Rosary in the car normal for them, so when they are ten or twelve years old, it will be normal to say, "We are going to the movies; on the way let's pray a Rosary."

Around the age of three, something special happens to children. They like to hear the story of Jesus. During your car Rosary or your evening family Rosary, take a moment to tell the story of Jesus in a substantial way at each mystery; instead of simply saying, "The First Sorrowful Mystery," tell them the story to the best of your ability in an age-appropriate way.

For example: "The First Sorrowful Mystery is the Agony of Jesus in the Garden. Jesus went out to a garden called Gethsemane. He knelt down to pray, but He was so sad and upset that His sweat turned to blood. He knew what was going to happen to Him, and when He looked for His friends, they were all asleep. Finally, the guards came to arrest Him." Then say, "Let's pray ten Hail Marys, and I will tell you the rest of the story." Children love this. They will patiently wait for you to pray ten Hail Marys to hear the rest. You are filling their little minds with the life of Christ and building in them the habit of prayer and compassion.

When praying the family Rosary with little children, be patient. They are kids. Often in a family Rosary, the youngest is very content to be with the family all in prayer, even if she isn't kneeling or sitting half the time. It is normal for children to move around and fidget and make noise. Let them do what they can as they grow and learn, perhaps saying the first few words of the Our Father or Hail Mary on their own, and then the family finishes for them. Tell them how much you love them and how happy you are to pray with them, no matter how it goes.

Maintain your own private devotion, and in your prayer, Mary will guide you and inspire you in the raising of your children. Investing in your children and the family Rosary while they are young is worth persevering through the difficulties.

> *There is no surer means of calling down God's*
> *blessing upon the family and especially of preserving*
> *peace and happiness in the home than the daily*
> *recitation of the Rosary. If this habit is inculcated*
> *into children at a young and impressionable age,*
> *they too will be faithful to the Rosary in later years.*
> —Ven. Pius XII[116]

Families with Teens

> *Because of the daily family Rosary, my home*
> *was for me a cradle, a school, a university, a*
> *library, and most of all, a little church.*
> —Ven. Patrick Peyton[117]

If you have persevered long enough in the family Rosary to have had infants grow into teens, you have been truly blessed. Day after day and year after year, these children have asked Our Lady to pray for them. These prayers are efficacious. Our Lady takes their hearts into her own; she loves them and will bless them for eternity for these prayers. Mary herself is guiding and equipping them for the work God has for their lives. During this time Our Lady has also been guiding and forming you, inspiring you and helping you to raise her children into future saints and soldiers of Christ. Keep going!

You have good children and holy teens, but teens are still teens. Obstacles and setbacks will arise. Persevere in your resolutions. Put your children in circumstances where they can be evangelized by others. Often young people take things more seriously when it comes from anybody but their parents. Put them in youth groups where the leaders promote the Rosary. Put them in places they will be encouraged to pray the Rosary even independent of family prayer time. Send them to youth conferences where the fire of their faith will be inflamed, and they will be encouraged to become saints. All the while, maintain your role as the primary educator of your children. The greatest thing a parent can teach their child is how to pray.

Teach them the ways of mental prayer. Young people are capable of deep prayer. In the family Rosary, begin to leave a little space where they have a moment to visualize the mystery and form an intention. Be sure to include a general family intention, but also allow the freedom for the family members to feel comfortable to include an intention. Have different family members take turns leading each decade, so they have some ownership. All of this need not take a long time. If you pray the vocal prayers at the pace that a normal human speaks to another person, communal prayer often takes twelve to fifteen minutes. Some families leave out the introductory prayers and just jump straight into the mysteries. Some families have additional devotions they add at the end, like a prayer to St. Michael or St. Joseph, which is all great. The key is to figure out what works for your family, have freedom, and be flexible. As your family evolves, how the family Rosary happens might also need to evolve.

As the children get older and begin to have after-school activities, or when a parent might be out for some obligation, always have a plan B. If half the family is at a school function and the other half is at home, make it clear the members at home will pray as usual and the group coming in later should pray the Rosary on the way home from the function. At some point, you will have a teen who is out on their own. God willing, when you ask them to please honor the family tradition and pray the Rosary, they will pray it on their own on that particular evening. I have seen that teens who honor Jesus and Mary will honor their father and mother when they are asked to pray the Rosary. In their heart of hearts, teens who have been praying since childhood realize they need God's help.

This requires diligence, but really it isn't as difficult as it seems if this is all flowing out of our own passionate relationship with God. Any effort is worth it. We can die in peace knowing we did all we could, and we can be at peace knowing that Mary will do all she can. In the worst-case scenario, if for whatever reason, your child goes off to college or out into the world and abandons Jesus and Mary, Mary doesn't abandon them. Once a child of Mary, always a child of Mary. She takes her motherhood very seriously. Our Lady never loses.

> *The fathers and mothers of families particularly*
> *must give an example to their children, especially*
> *when, at sunset, they gather after the day's work,*
> *within the domestic walls, and recite the Holy Rosary*
> *on bended knees before the image of the Virgin.*
> — Pope Pius XI[118]

Starting a New Devotion in Established Families or Nontraditional Situations

> *The Rosary can bring families*
> *through all dangers and evils.*
> —Ven. Patrick Peyton[119]

Now we will address the difficult situations. First, if you converted later in life or if you are just discovering the Rosary, there is the temptation to feel like you have failed your family. Be at peace. You did your best with what you knew at the time. Don't beat yourself up over things you can't change. Nothing is outside the providence of God; trust that your eyes opened at the right moment.

These recommendations are for introducing the family Rosary into a situation where the teens are older and most, if not all, of the family is opposed. This becomes even more difficult when a spouse is not on board. It is a steep hill to climb, but you must tackle it. We have an obligation to do everything possible to try and get our spouses and children to Heaven. This often means a lot of prayer and a lot of suffering, but again, this isn't outside of God's providence. This is how you will become a saint!

Focus on yourself first. Make sure that you have fully interiorized the Rosary. Let it take deep root in your soul. Make the intention of your Masses and Rosaries be to obtain grace for the members of your family.

In prayer, ask Mary to lead you and give you insight about your situation, because every circumstance is different. She will lead you. You could try the bulldozer approach: "This is what we are doing starting tomorrow." In most cases, it works only if both spouses are on board. More often, it is best to take Our Lord's advice to be as cunning as a serpent and as gentle as a dove.

Start by inviting people to pray a Rosary with you. For example, say, "I am going for a walk; will you come and pray the Rosary with me?" If they say no, don't be disturbed; you just planted a seed for a later opportunity. When your birthday comes around, you can try, "I would love it if we could all pray the Rosary, or even just a decade."

If your spouse is interested but unsure, discuss implementing a weekly Rosary. What this is doing is watering the soil. Everything is grace. Your constant intercession has been like calling in airstrikes upon enemy territory. The sacrifices and Rosaries you are offering are loosening the grip of the evil one and watering the soil of your family's souls with rain from Heaven. Then, when you get them to pray the Rosary, even just occasionally, they themselves call upon Mary. She begins to plant the seeds of faith. Even if they say their Hail Mary with resignation, Our Lady accepts it. The devil convinces people that for prayers to be effective, they have to be said with tears and emotion; this is a lie. Just pray.

Here comes the secret weapon: Advent and Lent. These are the perfect starting times for implementing the family Rosary. Now, after the soil has been broken and watered, you can start to yield a harvest. "This year for Lent we should pray the family Rosary." Not met with any enthusiasm? "Lent is about sacrifice. Offer it up!" During Lent and Advent, the entire mystical Body of Christ is making penance. Then, when Lent and Advent are over, everybody in the family has the grace to keep going. They are disposed and really want to keep praying the Rosary, but just lack the discipline.

Perhaps you are facing a worst-case scenario: You are all alone in your faith, and it seems like your spouse and children are against you. Yes, it is a battle, but you must fight. Nothing is as hopeless as it looks. So often, when a person takes up all the mysteries of the Rosary, at least one member of the family comes around. A tragedy strikes, and they are brought to their knees in humility before God.

Then the prayer of two is more powerful than just one. Try and find an ally who will pray with you, even on occasion. Pray with them as often as possible and strategically invite your spouse to pray. All of this is going to hurt; the rejection is going to hurt, and the penance is going to hurt. But with Our Lady, you will persevere. If you are reading this, be assured these words are meant for you. You have a moral obligation to fight for the souls of your spouse and your children. If you fight and are willing to die on your cross, with Mary, you will not lose.

> *Spiritually unite yourself to Jesus Crucified and*
> *trustfully abandon yourselves into the hands of Mary,*
> *calling upon her unceasingly with the Rosary.*
> — Pope Benedict XVI[120]

How Many Rosaries? One, Two, Three, Four, or More?

> *Most Holy Virgin, obtain for us the grace to*
> *devoutly pray your most holy Rosary.*
> — St. Anthony Mary Claret[121]

One of the most important plans we will make is our rule of life. This is a spiritual plan that, if followed, will help us to become a saint. How often should I go to Confession? How often should I go to Mass? How many Rosaries should I pray? These are all important questions that each person must discern.

I can't tell you how much to pray. If it comes from me, it won't last. Every person must take the question to prayer with an open heart. Before your next Rosary, ask her, "Blessed Mother, how many Rosaries do you want me to pray?" I promise, she will reveal it to you. It is so important that it comes from her. When you have that interior conviction, write it down.

Remember, when God gives consolation, when He speaks, He acts. If God convicts us to do something, He also gives us the grace to do it. I say pray with an open heart, because sometimes, if we are closed and don't really want to know God's will, He tends not to speak. Do God's will. That being said, I will give you a few suggestions to consider.

The Daily Rosary

If you are not praying the Rosary at all, I encourage you to just start with a single Rosary. This can be terribly difficult for some people. When you first start out, you may need to break it up at different points in the day and do one decade at a time.

Remember, if you haven't prayed, there is a spiritual battle also happening. As grace builds and as you develop the prayer muscle, you can pray a five-decade Rosary all at once. Don't compare yourself to others. Don't let your desire to be perfect keep you from doing something good. It is okay to pray badly, as long as you really are trying your best. The only bad Rosary is the one you didn't pray.

Only by prayer do you get better at prayer. Something is better than nothing. Praying one Rosary a day is truly life changing. If the desire to pray is from the Heart of God, don't let anybody sidetrack you. Guard this devotion with every fiber of your being. One caution in praying one Rosary is that, if you fail, you won't have prayed any Rosaries that day. For many people that means they might not have prayed at all. The devil will give us excuses to keep us from praying. He knows that if he can distract us from praying our daily Rosary, we forgo the protection of Our Lady and we are unarmed. Cling to Mary and beg for the grace to be faithful.

If you are currently already praying one Rosary a day, and you love it and are going strong, I encourage you, be open to change. It could be that Our Lady wants to stretch you, and she might ask you to increase, even for a season. One of the benefits of being a child of Mary is that she looks at our situation, she sees the needs of family and friends. It could be that one of our loved ones is in serious spiritual danger. Mary might want to help them, but she needs somebody to pray and sacrifice. She might be inviting us to more, so that grace can be obtained for an important intention.

Be open. Truly seek to be indifferent in your discernment. If you are called to more, she will help you to accomplish it. Everything is a grace.

Two or Three Rosaries per Day

If Our Lady is calling you to pray two or three Rosaries per day, be intentional about how many and when you are going to pray. The family Rosary could certainly count as your second Rosary for the day. One of the great things about planning on praying more than one Rosary a day is, if for some reason we fail on a given day, at least we got one or two done.

If you are praying two or three Rosaries per day, pray the mysteries for the day multiple times that day. So, if it is a Tuesday, pray the Sorrowful Mysteries all day. I recommend this for a few reasons. Firstly, it is easy to return to the same meditation that you already made and found fruitful. Second, by doing the mysteries of the day more than once, you ensure you get every aspect of Christ's life by the end of the week.

For some who resolve to pray three Rosaries a day, you might be tempted to do only the Joyful, Sorrowful, and Glorious Mysteries. You are free to do it this way, but I really believe that it is important to get the entire life of Christ in through the Luminous Mysteries, so following the mysteries that correspond with the days of the week is easiest.

A consistent comment from people who pray multiple Rosaries is that they find it easier to pray multiple Rosaries than to pray just one. I have found that this is true as well. Partly, it is practical. If you have planned to pray three Rosaries, you know if this is going to be successful, you have to get a Rosary done early, so there is less hesitation to jump in and get started.

There is also an element of spiritual warfare involved. When you pray the first Rosary, the graces from that first Rosary afford you protection and strength to pray more, which is a grace you didn't previously have. Many people find that praying three was way easier than they thought, and Our Lady calls them to more. The beauty is that, at this point, the grace is flowing in your life and recognizing Mary's tug on your heart becomes easier.

Four Rosaries: All the Mysteries

My brothers and sisters, if, while reading this chapter, you were waiting for me to get to this section on praying all four Rosaries every day, that might be a sign this is for you. If the chapter on the benefits and promises of the full Rosary captured your attention and got you excited, that is a sign this might be for you. If you are constantly in mortal sin or involved in spiritual warfare, I personally believe that the four Rosaries is for you. Living in the state of grace is a must. Finally, if you have a spouse, a child, or somebody you love who is by all objective standards not going to Heaven, I strongly encourage you to consider the four Rosaries. Our Lady doesn't impose this on anybody, but she is offering you an invitation to enter into a deeper relationship with her. Open your heart and ask her: "What do you want of me, Mother?"

I can say without hesitation that I recommend praying all the mysteries of the Rosary every day. This practice has radically and totally changed my life. Every good thing in my life, I owe to Our

Lady and the Most Holy Rosary. Our Lady has kept all her promises and given me far more than I could have ever asked for.

She delivered me from the hands of the devil. She took me in and accepted me as her own son. She has given me what I don't deserve, a ministry and a beautiful family. I have no doubt that without Mary and the Rosary, I would have ruined everything for everyone. Without her, I could still ruin it. She has protected me time and time again, not just from the devil, but from myself. She has helped me to overcome my vices. I promise, if you begin the practice of praying all the mysteries every day, she will do something similar for you. She will take you as her own, she will mold you, and she will organize your life.

If you are faithful to praying the Rosary, you will receive all the benefits and promises that Our Lady made to St. Dominic and Bl. Alan, as well as all those I have mentioned throughout this book. Our Lady keeps her promises, but we must be all in. You will overcome your vices. She will destroy the traps of the enemy and pour grace into your life, and that grace will overflow into the lives of your family members. Every aspect of your life will flourish. Your sacramental life will increase. Your charismatic gifts, knowledge, and love of God will increase.

This is not to say that crosses won't come; they most certainly will, but on our way of the cross, she will show us her face. She gives us a glimpse at the deeper purpose in our suffering. All things work for the good of those who love the Lord. How much more for the children of Mary? If you are called to pray all the mysteries of the Rosary, as an invitation or out of necessity, consider it one of the greatest blessings of your life. She wants to make you a saint. The two greatest fruits of praying the Rosary are peace of soul and holiness.

My brothers and sisters, *ask for the grace to be faithful to the Rosary*. It is a grace. One cannot climb this mountain by willpower alone. If you are resolved to pray the entire Rosary, don't pray it all in one sitting. Break it up evenly at fixed times. You will leave prayer with a renewed sense of the presence of God.

I also recommend that you pray the four sets of mysteries in chronological order so that you have a balanced look at the life of Christ. This isn't essential, but it is recommended. A friend might ask you to pray with them, and they want to pray a set of mysteries you already prayed; that is fine. During Holy Week, you may want to pray only the Sorrowful Mysteries that entire week. You have the freedom to do this. As long as, at the end of the day, you prayed four, Our Lady gives you the grace. There is a special grace that is given when you complete the four, precisely because you have answered her call to pray the Rosary. The whole is greater than the sum of its parts. The grace of having completed the full Rosary is greater than the sum of praying one Rosary four times.

Review the five tips noted earlier. Especially at first, be content with praying it poorly for a time, because you're building a habit. Our Lady is much like an athletic trainer; she will get you into shape. But first you have to show up at the appointed times for your workouts. All good things will flow from this regular encounter with Jesus, through Mary

More Than a Full Rosary per Day

Take a deep breath, because we are in the last category. You might find yourself in an extraordinary situation or in a season of life when Mary is calling you to more. You might have a major retreat coming up, a family member might be sick in the hospital, or for some other reason you are called to more. If this is you, she will convict you of it. She will provide the grace.

In general, we can take the attitude of, *I will pray the Rosary as often as possible,* meaning you have the Rosary always in your pocket, on your belt, or in your hand. Every free moment, you are praying a decade of the Rosary: walking to your car, waiting for your lunch, between classes, or while you are getting a haircut. Depending on the day, you may pray six or you might pray twelve. This is a beautiful practice that many of the saints utilized. You might not feel holier, you won't be walking on clouds, but the graces you obtain will be used by Mary for countless good works all over the world.

It is said that the prayers of the contemplative religious keep the earth from collapsing, and this is true also of Our Lady's prayer warriors. I have a friend who is suffering from Parkinson's disease. He can't always do what he wants, but he can pray. He intercedes for Our Lady's intentions with over twenty-four Rosaries a day. This is a special calling; be open to it. If this is you, please include me in your petitions.

> *If you release me from your Immaculate hands for*
> *even only one instant, I will be the first to fall into the*
> *most grievous sins and into the bottom of hell. But if*
> *you do not let go of me and will lead me, I will surely*
> *not fall and I will become a Saint, a great Saint.*
> — St. Maximilian Kolbe[122]

PROMOTE THE ROSARY

> *My only purpose in thirty-three years of service*
> *has been that of saving my soul and that of my*
> *brother by spreading the most holy Rosary.*
> — Bl. Bartolo Longo[123]

If you have read this book and you have long been a child of Mary and a devotee of the Holy Rosary, you are indebted to Our Lady. If you have read this book and are just now beginning this journey with Mary, you are indebted to Our Lady. The Lord on the Cross just before dying cried out, "I thirst." Jesus thirsts for souls. The fastest and most effective means for quenching Jesus' thirst is to promote the Rosary. The only way we can begin to repay Our Lady for what she has done for us is by assisting her in promoting the Rosary. The greatest act of charity we can do for our neighbor is to promote the Rosary. If you are fully committed to the Rosary, your devotion will naturally spill out into the lives of your family members, but here are some brief tips for sharing the Rosary beyond the four walls of your home.

1. Give away rosaries and pamphlets on how to pray the Rosary. People who receive rosaries as gifts are usually very appreciative. This rosary-giving can take many shapes depending on the situation. If you are giving a rosary to a fallen-away family member or close friend, I recommend purchasing a nice, high-quality rosary. You will feel the weight of this sacrifice, but so will the person receiving it. The quality, beauty, and generosity of your gift will be felt. If you make rosaries or even have cheaper plastic rosaries, these also make good gifts for friends and coworkers. Something is better than nothing. Again, don't let your desire to be perfect get in the way of a good deed.

Be sure to provide a pamphlet on how to pray the Rosary. The pamphlet is essential, or else a person who doesn't know how to pray will use their rosary as a keepsake only and not for prayer.

2. When somebody is suffering, encourage them to pray the Rosary. Witness to how the Rosary helped you in times of suffering. Offer to pray the Rosary with them. Suffering lowers our guard, and we are desperate for help when we are suffering. Encourage the Rosary, but also let them know you are going to offer a Rosary (or more) on their behalf. Grace helps!

3. Let your private devotion spill into other people's lives. Because you are always praying, you are always seen with a rosary in your hand or on your person. If you have the habit of praying the Rosary frequently at work, when going for walks, or in the car, invite your friends and coworkers to join you. Even if they aren't Catholic, make the offer. If they say no, ask them again when the Spirit prompts you. Often when people say no, they question themselves. Or something happens later and they think, "Well, if they ask again, I will say yes." The problem is we get so self-conscious that we never ask again. Don't be a pest, but bring it up from time to time.

4. Take advantage of social media. On occasion, post quotes and little testimonies on your social media pages. There are many people who never comment on our posts, but they see what we are posting. One day the right message will hit them. This can open the door for further evangelization.

5. Preach and teach about the Rosary. Volunteer to teach catechism and high school faith formation. Volunteer to give a talk or lesson on the power of the Rosary. If you don't, who will? When promoting the Rosary, pray the Rosary as a preparation. Our Lady will give you insights into what to speak about. She will also bless your efforts, and the Holy Spirit will make sure that this message falls on fertile soil.

> *If you wish to convert anyone to the fullness of the knowledge*
> *of Our Lord and of his Mystical Body, then teach him*
> *the Rosary. One of two things will happen. Either he will*
> *stop praying the Rosary or he will get the gift of faith.*
> —Ven. Fulton Sheen[124]

CONCLUSION

Thank you for reading this book. I have emptied my heart, and I am confident that if I have left anything out, Mary will answer all your questions in mental prayer. Her spouse, the Holy Spirit, will guide you in all truth. I want to leave you with one final encouragement: Say "yes." Say yes to God's will. Become the saint He created you to be. So many souls hang in the balance, waiting for the grace and influence from your yes. He has created you with a plan and a purpose. Saying yes to God's will isn't just the greatest adventure of your life, but it is the essence of sanctity. The surest guarantee that we will do God's will is with, in, and through Mary. Say yes to Mary, echo her fiat, and pray the Rosary every day.

I leave you with a prophecy from St. Louis de Montfort. May it be fulfilled in you.

> Almighty God and his holy Mother are to raise up great saints who will surpass in holiness most other saints as much as the cedars of Lebanon tower above little shrubs....
>
> These great souls filled with grace and zeal will be chosen to oppose the enemies of God who are raging on all sides. They will be exceptionally devoted to the Blessed Virgin. Illumined by her light, strengthened by her food, guided by her spirit, supported by her arm, sheltered under her protection, they will fight with one hand and build with the other.... By word and example they will draw all men to a true devotion to her....
>
> ... They will become, in Mary's powerful hands, like sharp arrows, with which she will transfix her enemies....
>
> They will be like thunder-clouds flying through the air at the slightest breath of the Holy Spirit. Attached to nothing, surprised at nothing, troubled at nothing, they

will shower down the rain of God's word and of eternal life....

Lastly, we know they will be true disciples of Jesus Christ, imitating his poverty, his humility, his contempt of the world and his love. They will point out the narrow way to God in pure truth according to the holy Gospel, and not according to the maxims of the world. Their hearts will not be troubled, nor will they show favour to anyone; they will not spare or heed or fear any man, however powerful he may be. They will have the two-edged sword of the word of God in their mouths and the blood-stained standard of the Cross on their shoulders. They will carry the crucifix in one hand and the rosary in the other, and the holy names of Jesus and Mary on their heart.[125]

CHAPTER 8

Testimonies of the Rosary

In this chapter I am providing a handful of testimonials. These testimonies are from people I know personally. Although I didn't go out seeking sensational stories, you will see in every account a consistent theme: the power of the Rosary.

RAISED ON THE ROSARY

I was taught to pray the Hail Mary and Our Father when I was three years old. The Rosary has had an integral place in my upbringing. I believe my life has been the way it has because of this simple prayer. Mary has protected me from so many of the horrors that plague the teenage world. I truly feel that the Rosary is the reason.

I am happy with my grades at school, my friendships, and my general well-being. I don't mean that I get whatever I want because I pray the Marian Psalter. But, whenever I offer my Rosary for a special intention, I know that the Virgin Mary will give me something more beneficial than what I asked for. She doesn't give me magic A's in school but the strength to keep studying. She doesn't give me first place in decathlon but the sportsmanship to accept my loss and the perseverance to try harder next year. She doesn't give me all the friends in the world but the right, good, Catholic peers that I need to stay strong in my faith.

I don't always sense the presence of Mary, but when I look back, I can clearly see she has been guiding my life. I am very grateful to God that I have been raised on the Rosary. I know that I'm still young, and that many challenges and sorrows will come my way, especially when I go into high school and college, but I know that Mary will help me through the good and the bad, even if I don't realize it at the time.

Gemma C. — student

THE ROSARY SAVED ME

Growing up, I found the Rosary long and monotonous, and I had little interest in it. My faith was minimal—Sunday Mass and prayers before meals. Though my parents sacrificed to send me to Catholic school, by the time I was in high school I saw the faith as merely a set of rules and not as a relationship with Jesus Christ. For the next decade, I embraced a worldly lifestyle, seeking happiness in partying and drinking. It was only after graduating college that I realized I was truly miserable.

At that time, my younger brother had rediscovered his faith, mainly through the Rosary. With guidance from a former teacher, he experienced a deep spiritual renewal. He urged me to turn back to God, persistently inviting me to pray with him.

Though resistant at first, I eventually agreed. Slowly, I saw the fruits—less desire for my old ways, more longing for Mass and Confession.

However, I fell back into sin and confided in my brother. He encouraged me to confess and take up a bold challenge: praying all four sets of mysteries of the Rosary daily. Initially hesitant, but ultimately I agreed. This decision radically changed my life forever. The Rosary opened my heart to God, igniting love for the Eucharist, Confession, and Adoration of the Blessed Sacrament. It granted me the peace I had long sought and strengthened me against temptation. Above all, it led me to hear God's call to the priesthood.

Today, as a seminarian, I continue to witness the Rosary's power. It has transformed my life, bringing me closer to Christ through Mary. The Most Holy Rosary should be a part of daily life for all Catholics, for through it we grow in love of God and neighbor, see His providence in all things, and ultimately are made into saints.

Keenan A.—seminarian

THE MIRACLE OF MY LIFE

Whatever growth I have accomplished in the spiritual life, I owe entirely to Our Lady and her Rosary. Whatever success I have had in abandoning sin and vice and growing in virtue and love, I credit to Mary and her Rosary. I have witnessed many miracles through Our Lady's Rosary. I've seen people healed of chronic, life-threatening diseases. And, more powerfully, I have witnessed countless spiritual healings and conversions through this humble prayer.

Maybe the greatest miracle I've witnessed through the Rosary is that of my own conversion—my own continued, daily conversion. The Rosary binds me to Jesus. When I developed the habit of praying all the mysteries each day, I discovered that the praise of Jesus and Mary are always on my lips and heart. Praying the entire Rosary fills the day with the sweet fragrance of God's presence.

The Rosary is the antidote to our pride. Each Ave Maria brings us into the mystery of the Incarnation—when God so humbled Himself even to becoming one of us. Some critics say the Rosary puts too much emphasis on Mary and not enough on Jesus. What foolishness! It would be easier to separate heat from the sun than to separate this Son from His Mother.

Our Lady's one goal is for us to be with her and her Son forever in Heaven. But there can be no growth in the spiritual life without a life a prayer. Here enters Our Lady's genius: We need tangible, physical assistance to pray. We are corporeal beings who do not know how to pray as we ought. And so, Our Blessed Lady has given us the key to her heart.

William D.—seminarian

MY PARENTS' GREATEST GIFT

I give honor and deepest gratitude to my parents for raising me Catholic, and particularly for teaching me how to pray the Rosary. It was through the family Rosaries we prayed and the visits to Our Lady's grotto after Holy Mass that I grew up knowing I am not only their child—I belong to God and to Mama Mary.

During my sophomore year of high school, I experienced a deep conversion through a school outreach project. An encounter with a poor child pierced my heart and moved me to ask some very hard questions: What is God calling me to do? How should I be living my life? In wrestling with these questions, I started to cling to my Rosary. This prayer has become my refuge and my weapon. It has become my favorite prayer.

When I pray the Rosary, I sense that my heart starts to beat with the Hearts of Jesus and Mary. In the rhythm of the prayers, I find peace and strength. In the contemplation of the mysteries, I find wisdom and obedience. Our Lady takes care of me and forms me to be like her Son. I know I am not the same after praying the Rosary.

Without the Rosary, it would have been hard to hear Jesus calling me to my religious vocation, and even harder to give my fiat. I want Jesus to become "the breath, the soul and the 'all' of my life," and I have found that the Rosary is a prayer that helps me to persevere in this desire.

I pray Our Lady helps us to always trust and have confidence, as we each live our vocation and mission. And I pray that Her Immaculate Heart be always our life, our sweetness, and our hope!

Sr. Chiara

Put Out into Deep Water

The Holy Rosary is Mary's net for snaring souls. As Jesus commanded Peter to lower his nets for a catch (see Luke 5:4), Mary invites us to have confidence that through the Rosary she can capture souls and bring them the healing grace they need from God.

Whenever I see a special need, have an important intention, or encounter someone marked by suffering, confusion, or alienation from God, I unwind the net of the Rosary and ask the Mother of God to go to work. Only a true mother could do this. Mary is our mother, not by analogy, but by our having been made children of God in Baptism. She is interested in each one of us as if we were her only child.

How could we not turn to her in confidence to give our love, to express our thanks, and to ask for her intercession?

Fr. Peter

The Seed My Grandmother Planted

My oldest memory of the Rosary goes back to when I was six years old. My maternal grandmother lived with us, and I remember seeing her every day, sitting in her cozy chair and silently praying her red rosary beads. She sat there for hours, praying and taking in the day.

As I grew in my faith, the Rosary sounded boring to me. How could someone just sit and recite the same prayers over and over? It wasn't until I became a parent and was faced with the task of raising children that the seed my grandmother had planted in my early childhood began to bear fruit. But even then, I never seemed to be consistent. When I told the priest about this in Confession, he encouraged me to keep trying and to pick a specific time in order for it to become a routine.

Now I play an audio Rosary on a loop as I cook dinner, do laundry, or clean the house. It brings me peace and hope. If worries creep into my day, I immediately turn to the Blessed Mother and start a Rosary. It's like a soothing balm. Each time I pick up my grandmother's red rosary beads, I am grateful Our Blessed Mother gave me the grace to experience the power of the Rosary.

Rebecca F. —grandmother, receptionist

THE ROSARY LED US HOME

In 2022, my family relocated from the Twin Cities to a small town in the middle of nowhere. It was a painful trial for me to embrace, for it meant leaving our wonderful parish, our friends, our community, and everything we held dear. And fitting into a new Catholic community turned out to be much more difficult than we had anticipated.

It was a deeply lonely time for me. We had three children under the age of four, and I no longer had friends or support. One of the greatest aches was that the nearest Adoration chapel was a half hour away. We had always lived close to Perpetual Adoration, and I loved my holy hour and being able to stop by throughout the week. I prayed every day to move back.

Two years later, my husband was unexpectedly offered a job as headmaster at a wonderful Catholic school back in the Twin Cities. I was elated! The day we put our house up on the market, Mary prompted me to offer up the selling of our home and the finding of a new home to her through a Miraculous Rosary Novena. My husband and I immediately began to pray.

Weeks and then months passed, and we still hadn't sold our home. We had several potential buyers, but something always popped up right before or after they made an offer. It was incredibly disheartening, but I trusted Mary knew what she was doing. Eventually we realized it was not the Lord's time, and we pulled our house off the market.

Many months passed and spring finally arrived. And then, out of nowhere, our prayers were answered: Our new parish owns a home that is steps away from the church, and the family living there decided it was time to move. The home was ours! And the best part? I can walk to the Perpetual Adoration chapel!

Even when all is dark and confusing and desolate, Mary is quietly and tenderly sorting things out for her children. Always entrust yourself to Our Lady through the Rosary. She will never fail you!

Brittany M. — wife, mother, and musician

THE 54-DAY ROSARY NOVENA CHANGED MY LIFE

In college we had a priest from Africa visit our school. He implored us to spend time with Jesus for thirty minutes every day as a Lenten resolution. That seemed like a very long time to me; at that point I was focused more on scheduling Jesus into my week with group prayer and bible studies. I decided that I could fill up at least twenty of those minutes with the Rosary.

I missed the first couple days of Lent and then remembered my resolution. I went to one of our campus chapels. I didn't know all the Rosary prayers, so I pulled up an audio recording and followed along. I was so excited when I completed that first Rosary on my own! As I sat there, I recalled that a famous Catholic speaker had mentioned she prayed a 54-Day Rosary Novena. I quickly Googled "54 Day Rosary Novena" and discovered that on February 16, 1884, Fortuna Agrelli started the very first 54-day novena. And there I was, sitting in that college chapel . . . on February 16! I knew at that moment I was being invited to pray a Rosary every day, not just for the forty days of Lent, but for fifty-four days.

My whole life changed. The prayers of the Rosary brought me into a deeper contemplation and intimacy with Jesus and Mary than I ever thought possible. In those short days of Lent, I began going to daily Mass and regular Confession, and the fire of evangelization burned greatly in my heart. The Virgin Mary has been my best friend ever since. Her beads are always in my hand.

Claire A. — youth minister

An Anchor for My Soul

In 2013, a couple of years before entering the seminary, I was inspired by the Holy Spirit to start praying the Rosary every day. I was a young man entering his twenties and living with many worldly ideas; however, after starting to pray that one daily Rosary, I experienced many graces, and many sins and sinful thoughts lost their grip on my life. The longer I stayed with it, the more I came to love Our Lord Jesus; soon, daily Mass, regular Confession, and eucharistic Adoration became part of my daily routine during college. It was also during these months that I started to discern the priesthood. Thanks to the intercession of Our Lady, the Rosary helped me to hear God's call in my life.

I entered seminary in 2015. The years 2020 and 2021 were challenging for me. In addition to the pandemic, I was suffering from a chronic illness that health care professionals didn't know how to cure. There was also a darkness in my soul that impacted my vocational discernment. Eventually, a friend, who I consider a brother, encouraged me to pray the full Rosary daily. Four sets of mysteries each day.

It is not an exaggeration to say that this prayer habit changed my life. I was completely healed from my illness, and I was healed from many spiritual wounds that I didn't even know I had. I have now been a priest for two years, and I can testify that praying the full Rosary daily has been an anchor and a strength in my vocation. I encourage everyone to try to pray the full Rosary, especially seminarians, priests, and consecrated religious. I know it sounds hard, but believe me, it is worth it. The four Rosaries will change your life!

Fr. Mauricio

A Methodist Meets Mary, One Bead at a Time

I was a pastor of a small United Methodist church when I prayed the Rosary for the first time. A lifelong Methodist, my curiosity about the Virgin Mary began while attending a Protestant seminary. Seeing her referenced in the classical writings of church history, I found myself stirred into a newfound appreciation for the Blessed Mother that slowly developed into a sincere devotion.

Before praying my first Rosary, I felt like someone about to leap into a cold shower, short of breath and beset with anxiety. What would my Methodist parishioners think if they caught me? Nevertheless, I went for it. More than twenty years later, and now a fully initiated Catholic, the Rosary has been the staple of my devotional life.

The Rosary has immersed me in the Gospels like nothing else ever has. Meditating on each mystery, I see how the Virgin Mary is the archetype of every disciple; that the New Testament itself paints our union with Christ in Mariological colors. At the Annunciation, Mary emptied herself and assumed the form of a servant (see Phil. 2:7). She was the good and immaculate soil upon which the divine Word fell, and nurturing it, produced an abundance (see Luke 8:15). Mary could truly say with St. Paul, "It is no longer I who live, but it is Christ who lives in me" (Gal. 2:20). Mary welcomed with meekness the implanted Word (see James 1:21); offered her body as "a living sacrifice" (Rom. 12:1); and bore the fruit of the Holy Spirit as a person (see Gal. 5:22). Before the Lord could offer His Body to us, it was Mary who first offered her body to Him.

The Rosary allows me to ponder with Mary the mystery of her incarnate Son. I have become a better Christian, a better evangelist, and a better man because of it.

Shane P. — husband, father, evangelist

I Started by Just "Getting It Done" — Then Mary Transformed Me

We make time for what we prioritize. For many years I didn't have time for the daily Rosary, but when, in a moment of desperation, I made time for four ... everything changed! I wasn't even good at praying the Rosary at first — I started out by just "getting them done." But then, through the Rosary, Mother Mary helped me fall in love with Our Lord in the Eucharist. I felt drawn to Confession and Adoration on a regular basis. She brought a peace to my soul and to my family that wasn't there before. I received many signal graces.

My crosses have not gone away, but I have such joy now. I know I can bear all things with her by my side; when I pray the Rosary, I know she is there with me.

Carolyn B. — wife, mother, teacher

A Priest with a Rosary Can Touch Every Soul

In high school, I was lost. I went to church on Sunday but would just go through the motions. Something was missing. I felt a gnawing uncertainty and a sense of emptiness that I couldn't shake.

At one point, in darkness and confusion, I asked the Lord for help. Then I stumbled upon *The Secret of the Rosary* by St. Louis de Montfort. Something began to stir in me, a gentle yet firm conviction to pray the Rosary daily. I decided to give it a shot, and things started to change. The pull toward sin weakened. The truths of the faith came alive. I started frequenting the sacraments. Our Lord became the center of my life.

Looking back, without the Rosary, I would be utterly lost. Now that I am a priest, my commitment to pray the entire Rosary daily (Joyful, Luminous, Sorrowful, and Glorious Mysteries) continues to be the game changer in my vocation and priestly ministry. As a priest, I cannot give what I do not have. By praying the entire Rosary and meditating on the mysteries daily, the gospel is preached in the silence of my heart every single day.

As a priest, I cannot save souls without grace. By praying the entire Rosary daily with my own personal intentions, I can touch any heart with supernatural grace: youth discerning their vocation, those who struggle with addictions, the dying as they prepare to meet the Lord, etc. As a priest, many things are out of my control, but no soul is out of my reach with the Rosary. I have seen firsthand the power of the Rosary. It has the power to change lives. It changed mine.

Fr. Josemaria

PEACE, HEALING, AND GRACE: THE POWER OF THE ROSARY

I went to Catholic school from pre-K through high school, and we went to Mass every Sunday. I never really strayed from my faith, but as I grew closer to Christ, it became clear that something was missing. I had never truly explored a relationship with Mary, Our Blessed Mother.

Shortly after turning thirty, I found myself praying in front of a statue of Our Lady and asking, "Mary, I want to know you more. How do I know you better?" I soon heard about a Marian pilgrimage that led me to complete my first Marian consecration. Though I didn't fully understand it at the time, it opened my heart to countless graces. I have now devoted my entire life, family, friends, and being to Our Lady. Out of deep love and gratitude, I've made the promise to pray the Rosary daily—and Mary has not disappointed.

Since committing to the Rosary, my life—and the lives of many family members and friends—has been revived by grace. My older brother, who hadn't stepped foot in a church in seventeen years, called my mom and asked if she'd meet him at church to pray the Rosary. My older sister, another cradle Catholic, was brought to her knees by a cancer diagnosis. In her pain, Mary was all she had to cling to. Now she's healed in more ways than one, prays the Rosary daily, visits the Blessed Sacrament with her two young kids, and shares Mary's healing with others. My mom now attends daily Mass, prays the Rosary, and radiates patience, selflessness, and love. Even my dad, who isn't Catholic and hasn't attended Mass in years, completed a Marian consecration with me. He often asks for Mary's intercession and places his worries in her hands. My niece and nephew, raised with no faith, ask to pray the Rosary with us over FaceTime. My niece has said, "Praying the Rosary makes me feel at peace in a way I've never felt before."

None of this was happening before the Rosary. It brings peace, healing, and endless graces. Be bold and ask Mary to help you know her, and she will answer in unexpected ways. Open your heart to her love, and you will be forever transformed.

Ellen M. — nurse

In the Night I Heard a Voice

When he was fourteen years of age, my dad — who was raised atheist — converted to the Faith. He always brought us to Sunday Mass. When I turned ten, we moved, and life changed. Dad tried his best, but circumstances defeated his efforts. I remember enjoying Mass, but that too faded.

Family life became quite dysfunctional. We (four girls) were country street kids with little family life to speak of. For a month, my sister and a friend used a Ouija board. I tried it once, but it scared me, so I stopped. Later, my sister began talking about demons — in our home, entering her body. Along with my siblings, I saw signs of demonic influence, but my parents ignored it. She had her first breakdown at nineteen. It was a long, hard road.

By my twenties, I rejected God, which led to poor choices and serious sin. At thirty, I married a Catholic and believed life would get better. It didn't. Over time, I discovered that our family history was riddled with tarot cards, palm reading, séances, horoscopes, ghost hunting — all of it. Yes, Satan's heyday.

One night, I woke up a mess. I took the rosary into bed and held it, having no clue how to pray it. Then I heard a clear, distinct voice from deep inside me: "I will help you." I sat straight up, shocked. I wondered, *What was that?* I didn't know. I thought maybe it was Jesus. I had no understanding of Mary or her role. It never occurred to me that it could be her.

Over time, I came to know Mary's voice. Through her Rosary, she began leading me, in the smallest of baby steps, to her Son. Many Rosaries later, I am a devoted wife, mom, and grandmother. My singular goal is to have the Holy Family with me as I pass from this life into the arms of Jesus. Mama Mary did for me as she desires to do for everyone, which is to lift us up to her Son.

Rose S. — wife, mother, grandmother

THE ROSARY MADE ME A REAL MAN

I had been trying to overcome porn for about fifteen years. The last five of those years, I got more serious about breaking it. I told people, formed accountability groups, read articles, and went to therapy. Gradually things improved, but it wasn't until I began praying the Rosary that things really began to change.

It all began when my friend showed me a talk online about the power of the Rosary. I was like, *Wow, maybe I should pray the Rosary*. I eventually committed to praying two Rosaries a day, asking Mary to pray for me to receive the grace to be chaste and to be the man God wants me to be. In just a short time, I noticed that the temptations had subsided enormously — and I was able to give up spending "free time" on the computer as well.

The time I spend with the Lord is time well spent. In the evening, I pray the Rosary with my wife and two young children. I have also started a men's group at my church and have started weekly Adoration at my school. I am positive that the Holy Spirit is working through me because of the time I have spent in prayer. Mary has been my spiritual Mother, and when I went to her looking to escape porn, she returned the favor by taking it away and giving me the courage to be a more loving father and a leader in my community.

I know I am capable of falling back into porn, but I do not fear it. I know I can seek the Lord's forgiveness and lean into the loving embrace of Mary. I will just keep praying the Rosary daily until I die. I am so thankful to Mary for the love she has for us.

Paul S. — husband, father, teacher

FROM BEAD TO BEAD, BACK TO CHRIST

The Rosary has helped me remain focused on the mysteries of Jesus Christ, especially when I find myself veering off course. It is in those moments when I start going from bead to bead that I find myself moving back to a life focused on Jesus Christ through the intercession of Our Blessed Mother and St. Joseph.

Fr. Preston

THE ROSARY REVEALED MY VOCATION

On my seventeenth birthday, I resolved to pray four Rosaries each day for the rest of my life. I would be lying if I said I was perfectly faithful to this resolution at first, but even in my inconsistency, Mary poured many graces into my life.

Within the first few months of praying four Rosaries a day (or at least trying to), Mary also began to reveal to me my own desire to be a priest, a desire that had been latent within my heart for several years. As I continued to pray the Rosary, this desire increased. The usual anxiety, doubt, and fear that so often cause young men to shrink from applying to seminary did not touch me, and I attribute this all to the Virgin Mary.

Using the sword that she placed in my hand, she slew every dragon in my path before I even knew they were there. Now, a few years into my priestly training, I have a deep relationship with Jesus Christ and a love for Him that increases each day, not because of any excellence of my own, but because of the Virgin Mary and her Holy Rosary.

Shawn V.—seminarian

From Jehovah's Witness to Mary's Child

When in 2022 I left the Jehovah's Witnesses and became Catholic, I continued to struggle to connect with the Blessed Mother. Even a year later, I thought the Rosary was too long, repetitive, and a waste of time. So, when I was challenged to pray the full Rosary for ten days, I hesitated. But I accepted—and what I once saw as a tedious prayer became a source of healing. The Rosary not only strengthened my faith but uncovered wounds I had buried for years.

As I meditated on each mystery, I saw myself more clearly— my struggles, my fears, my need for God's grace. It became my refuge, drawing me into a deeper relationship with Christ. I began attending Mass and Adoration daily, and with each prayer, my heart softened.

Now, two years later, I can't imagine my life without it. I teach religious education to young children, constantly reminding them to pray for the Virgin Mary's intercession. Who would have thought I would develop a devotion to the Blessed Mother? Yet, through the Rosary, I have consecrated myself to the Miraculous Medal. In moments of fear, I invoke her presence by praying these five words aloud: *Hail Mary, full of grace.* Instantly, all fear disappears.

Praying the Rosary has given me a faith in God I never knew I needed. It has transformed my heart, mind, and soul. What once seemed meaningless is now the prayer that changes everything.

Gladys V. — teacher

THE ROSARY SAVED MY MARRIAGE

As a newlywed I had not anticipated my husband choosing to skip attending Sunday Mass with me. "I'll never become Catholic. I don't want to be labeled," he said.

He was raised Protestant and seemed to have a good relationship with God, so I tried to understand. But I felt lonely and ashamed going to Mass alone. I'd get angry at him, and he'd get angry back, and each Sunday was filled with pain instead of God's glory. I tried everything to resolve the problem: I tried to understand. I tried not to care. I tried to convert to his ideologies. I tried to fix myself. I tried to fix him. And when I'd tried it all, I'd repeat the cycle.

Then, in 2020, after a pilgrimage to Birmingham, Alabama, I committed to saying one Rosary every day for the next year. And in 2021, just before my husband left for a business trip, our marriage unraveled. The hurt was so deep I couldn't see a way out, and it looked like we would have to go separate ways. While he was away, I was sick at heart. In a moment of torrential tears, I cried to God, "Please, Lord, if you want my marriage, I need you to heal it. I completely surrender it all to you."

My husband returned from his trip and asked me to sit down; he had something to tell me. After all we had been through, I should have felt fear. Instead, I could feel that something had changed.

"I'm shocked," he said somberly. "I'm becoming Catholic."

In the next six months, he sped through RCIA and was welcomed into the Catholic Church! This all coincided with the one-year mark of my doing the Rosary for a year! Now we both pray the full Rosary every day! God has continued to bless our marriage with graces, as we grow closer to Him.

Michelle C. — wife

WHY I PRAY THE ROSARY IN THE CAR

Years ago, I drove to a senior living community to visit a priest living there. I really enjoyed these visits. He had beautiful, holy images and books in his room, which sparked conversations about saints, like St. Joseph and St. Padre Pio, and about Catholic churches in the area. As our visits came to an end, he always found a way to mention the Rosary.

At the end of one visit, I said, "Father, I've got to get on the road and drive home." He asked how far; I responded, "About twenty-five minutes." He said, "Good, just enough time for you to pray the Rosary."

Driving home on the freeway, I decided to take his advice and began praying the Rosary. On that drive, suddenly, two lanes to my left and just ahead of me, a mattress flew off the bed of a pickup truck and became airborne, tumbling across the freeway. Cars began honking and swerving. As the mattress flew directly toward me, I couldn't slow down or change lanes.

Miraculously, the mattress landed directly in front of my car — centered perfectly, so that I drove over it without touching any part of it. I truly believe this was the strong signal I needed to understand the power of the Rosary and Our Lady's protection.

Deandra T. — mother, instructor

FINDING PEACE FROM DEPRESSION

February 7, 2023, marks the day that my life changed completely. I watched a video about the power of praying the whole Rosary—all four mysteries—every day. I thought, *Why not? I'll try it for seven days.*

Years later, I'm still doing it. I used to suffer from crippling depression and anxiety since middle school. It was brutal. As I got older and became a wife and mother, my faith grew, and I frequented the sacraments often, but I would still endure bouts of terrible depression, anxiety, and anger. Everything in my life seemed like a nonstop struggle.

Literally, the first day that I prayed all four Rosaries, it was like a shield of protection went up and all of my emotional troubles went away. Bead by bead, I tap into so many graces and experience such a tremendous love for God, Mary, the sacraments, and my family. I have changed into a much more peaceful and loving person.

All glory to God!

Erin D.—*wife, mother of six*

THE ROSARY CONNECTS ME TO JESUS

The Rosary is so much more than just repeating Hail Marys and Our Fathers; it is a deep meditation on the mysteries of Christ's life. When I pray the Rosary, I feel more connected to Jesus—especially in the Sorrowful Mysteries. As I pray these mysteries, it's as though I am there with Him, consoling *Him.* In those moments, I know He sees me, even in my darkest and deepest struggles. I realize He endured His Passion for me personally, to save me. That understanding, that connection, is beyond words.

Another grace I've experienced is how the Rosary unlocks the mysteries of Scripture. The more I meditate on Christ's life, the more the Bible comes alive. From His baptism in the Jordan, echoing Elijah calling down fire from Heaven, to Our Lady as the New Eve — there's an incredible depth waiting to be discovered.

The Rosary is one of the most biblical devotions we have. I highly recommend it to anyone seeking deeper faith and a closer relationship with Christ.

Gian Carlo A. — husband, father, entrepreneur

SOBER BY GRACE

For years, I struggled to control my alcohol consumption, repeatedly falling into a cycle of overindulgence. All that changed one night — just before Father's Day — when I went out with the guys, drank excessively, and returned home inebriated. My wife confronted me, and what followed was the darkest moment of my life. Consumed by alcohol and anger, I lashed out in a verbal rage, terrifying my wife and waking our children.

That night, she made the painful but necessary decision to ask me to leave.

Lost and broken, I turned to the only place I knew could hold me — our parish's 24/7 Adoration chapel. Night after night, I knelt before the Blessed Sacrament, pouring out my heart, clinging to my Rosary, and begging for mercy. A week into my exile, I added prayers to St. Jude and began the Surrender Novena, desperately offering my life into God's hands.

On the ninth day of the novena, after finishing my Rosary, everything changed. A grace beyond understanding washed over me, and in an instant, the craving for alcohol disappeared. It was gone — completely, miraculously gone.

Today, I am nine months sober. I am back home, and through God's mercy, my marriage is not only healing but stronger than it has been in years. I stand in awe of the miracle Christ has worked in my life. To Him, through the intercession of Our Blessed Mother and St. Jude, I give all my gratitude and praise.

Austin S. — husband, father

FROM LUKEWARM TO LEADING MY FAMILY

Growing up as a cradle Catholic, my faith was little more than Sunday Mass. My family did not pray together, and by high school, I had drifted into the sins and distractions of the world. Even after I married my wife and we started a family, I remained spiritually complacent — until I discovered the daily Rosary.

I had become deeply troubled by the moral decay in the world but felt powerless to change it. Then, I met a friend through our parish who promoted praying the full Rosary. At first, I thought praying fifteen or twenty decades a day was extreme, but as I started with five decades, I felt drawn deeper.

Over time, I committed to praying the full Rosary daily. Slowly but surely, grace transformed me. Mortal sins that once seemed insurmountable vanished. My love for the sacraments deepened, I wanted to confess my sins more frequently, and I found myself leading my family in prayer.

The rosary didn't just change my habits — it changed my heart. I developed a hunger for holiness, a love for the Church, and a desire to be the spiritual leader my family needed. Today, I cannot imagine life without this devotion. If you desire true conversion, pray the Rosary daily. It will transform you.

Chris M. — husband, father

FROM TRAUMA TO TRIUMPH

What began as a pilgrimage on spring break 2024 — traveling to St. Helena's Church in Amite, Louisiana, to pray for my husband's health, our finances, our children, and our faith — became a journey of miracles. That morning at the church, we received a priest's blessing and left renewed, carrying two Virgin Mary statues — one for a friend, Rosario, and one for our home.

Hours later, on our way home, our lives changed forever when an eighteen-wheeler shattered our peace. I'll never forget the sound of my daughter's screams piercing the air. My husband, son, and daughter were rushed to the nearest trauma center. Quickly I retrieved the statues from our wrecked car, which had been leaning behind my daughter's seat.

At the hospital, I stood trembling, torn between my children's exam rooms. My son, through tears, begged me to promise that God would let his sister walk again. I was paralyzed, unable to speak. In desperation, I silently prayed the Hail Mary — the one prayer that had always calmed me. As talks of ICU transfer arose, my son pleaded to pray with his sister. Together they began the Rosary, a practice we often turned to in times of despair. In that moment, I felt a deep warmth, as if the Blessed Mother was telling me our blessings would come through the Rosary.

Word spread, and people far and near joined us in praying the Rosary. Miracles unfolded. Through God's grace and Mary's intercession, our daughter was healed. Not only did she walk again — she now plays soccer at a national level! Looking back, I can see so many little signs of God's grace upon us. And now, no matter where we are, we continue to pray the Rosary as a family.

Ive C. — wife, mother

A Rosary Love Story

I became Catholic before I got married; I wanted to share the same faith with my husband. Up to that time, I was never involved with any church and had no personal relationship with Jesus. But even after I was confirmed in the Faith, I lived a sinful life and was not a good example for my kids.

In 2020, my daughter started associating with a bad group of friends. I sought the advice of a friend who had faced hard times in the past. She told me I needed to pray the Rosary. At the time, I didn't know how. So I looked up Rosary prayers on YouTube and started praying along every morning. Within the month, I started having this thirst to know God better. It was a love story that unfolded.

I began volunteering at our church—teaching elementary faith formation, helping with youth night, and teaching Confirmation to high school kids. I gave a presentation on the Rosary at youth night to promote praying it and have consecrated myself to Mother Mary.

My newfound love for God can only be explained by praying the Rosary. Mary has given me this unexplainable fervor for Jesus that I had never had before—and I am grateful for it.

Jenny H.—wife, mother, optometrist

Fall in Sin or Rise in Prayer

As a Catholic, I've learned two important spiritual lessons.

The first lesson is this: In order to refrain from sin, I need to be in a constant state of prayer. I am broken, and I need God's help.

The second lesson is just as important: The devil cannot be in the presence of the Blessed Virgin Mary.

Once I understood these two important lessons, the way of the Rosary made complete sense to me. I wanted to be always in the presence of Our Lady, so the devil had no influence over me. And above all, I wanted to stop sinning—and I knew I was too broken and weak to do it on my own.

So, I took up the Rosary in earnest. Now, praying the Rosary wasn't something I picked up in a day, or even in a week. It took time. It was hard. But when I devoted myself to it, meaning I prayed it even when I didn't want to, something happened: Grace came into my life in a way I can't fully explain.

I was able to refrain from sins that once conquered me. Grace felt visible. I could see God moving. I became a better person, brother, son, and friend. For me, the Rosary is like a sword against the devil and a ladder to Heaven.

I still fail. I fail to pray—and when that happens, I sin. I can literally see the fruit of the Rosary in how my life goes depending on whether I pray it or not.

I truly mean it when I say: The person who does not give up on the Rosary will see its fruits. The Rosary is extremely powerful. It's the love of our Mother. The person who becomes aware of Mary's love cannot help but feel called to holiness!

Sebastian V.—counselor

MARY IS CARRYING ME THROUGH MS

Like many people, I was born Catholic but left the Church during my high school years. I took whatever graces I had and ran with them. Continuing to make the same mistakes, I eventually joined a Baptist church, believing that I alone could "figure it out."

During 2020, with time on my hands, I decided to give the Church I had left another chance. I looked into it. I found many similarities with what I had been taught, but nothing that truly pulled me back.

That's when I first encountered Rosary talks on YouTube. The speaker's words encouraged me.

I began to pray the Rosary—sheepishly—just one a day. But things progressed quickly. Soon, I found myself praying all four sets of mysteries every day. At that point, all the graces and confidence I needed to formally return to the Church were there. I went to my first Confession in over twenty years, in tears. After that, my heart was on fire—for the Blessed Virgin Mary, her divine Son, and the Rosary.

Around that time, I was diagnosed with MS, so I leaned heavily on Mary and the Rosary. No breath could be wasted. I prayed back-to-back Rosaries all day, only stopping to eat and use the washroom. Eventually, I was praying an unimaginable number of Rosaries a day. I needed this. My Mother comforted me so much through this that it would not have been possible to survive without her constant consolation.

During that time, I went from being partially paraplegic to being able to walk fifty meters with no assistance. I never set out to pray the Rosary, but I just love it, and I love *her*, so much. Ave Maria.

Brian D. — prayer warrior

COMPRESSION SOCKS AND CONSOLATION

I have been coping with health issues since the birth of my child several years ago. One of these issues was heart palpitations. Frequent, disturbing, and at times painful, they had no discernible pattern of onset in relation to stress, emotions, or physical activity. I was also experiencing pelvic pain and leg swelling. I was only in my thirties, yet I felt like my health was falling apart.

A couple years ago, my husband and I started to experience a deep renewal in our Catholic Faith. Looking back, I cannot explain this in any other way than that the Holy Spirit moved within us. The following year, I started to feel compelled to pray the Rosary, a prayer I used to pray daily as a child but would later pray perhaps just twice a year on the anniversary of a grandparent's death. But that summer, restless in my mind and heart, I finally resolved to pray the Rosary every single day.

Within weeks, I realized that the palpitations had disappeared. I also realized I no longer needed to wear compression socks every day at work; the leg swelling had resolved. Eventually, I recognized that these inexplicable recoveries were miracles from God, starting not long after my daily devotion to the Most Holy Rosary.

The Rosary has provided for me a sense of calmness I never knew I was missing and can no longer envision myself living without. Thank God for the Rosary, for His Mother, and for His Divine Mercy.

Christine D. — wife, mother

DECADES AND DIAPERS

The work of a mother of five little kids, ages seven and under, can often feel anything but "holy." How can this very messy vocation possibly give You glory, God?

During my pregnancy with baby number five, I was physically sick and spiritually dry. I felt like I couldn't pray, I couldn't read, I could barely get off the couch ... all I could do was pray the Rosary. It was during this time that I was led to a YouTube video on the power of praying the entire Rosary. A fire was lit in my soul, and my life has never been the same. I started praying all twenty mysteries of the Rosary every single day, and Our Blessed Mother transformed my life into something more beautiful than I could have imagined.

When I turn to her, Mary takes the seemingly mundane tasks and turns them into encounters with her Son. As I wash dishes, fold laundry, nurse a baby, clean up spills, drop off kids at school, with each decade of the Rosary I unite myself to Our Lady, and she offers those acts to God. It is a sanctifying moment, for the more I unite myself to her, the more she molds my heart to be like hers.

With each decade I become more patient, more loving, more attentive; the sacrifices of motherhood don't feel so burdensome. Even when it's chaos all around me, I remember the words of St. Maximilian Kolbe: "I see Mary everywhere. I see difficulties nowhere." If you're a mom in the trenches of motherhood with lots of littles and you feel unseen, take heart! Our Lady sees you and loves you! Ask her for the grace to start praying the entire Rosary every single day. She will never fail to give you that grace, and she will bring a sweetness to your life that only she can give.

Hannah G. — wife, mother

The Fall that Should Have Killed Me

I come from a very broken family. My mother abandoned me due to alcoholism when I was four, and I entered the foster care system. At age six, I was adopted. My parents didn't raise me with any faith, but I converted to Catholicism at nineteen. Around that time, I joined the Marine Corps and served as an infantryman from 2006 to 2010. Though I rarely practiced, the Faith stayed with me.

I never prayed the Rosary or asked for Mary's intercession — until September 2020, when I came across several YouTube videos promoting the Rosary. I said, "What do I have to lose?" I picked up my old rosary and promised Mary that I'd pray it every day. And my faith life took off like a rocket.

One day, while working construction on a sheet metal roof, I was wearing a harness but hadn't clipped in so I could help my coworker. As I stepped across a gap onto a stack of panels, they shifted beneath me—and I fell thirty-five feet to the concrete below, landing on my pelvis and shattering my hip. Panels crashed down like flying guillotines, hitting the ground so hard they left deep indentations—right next to me. My hard hat stayed on but split down the middle.

I should have died. I should be paralyzed. But I wasn't. The rosary was in my pocket when I fell. As I held my rosary in the hospital, I knew: Mary had interceded. She saw my efforts to amend my life and asked her Son to save me.

Today, I walk normally. I feel no pain. I will never stop praying or promoting the Rosary.

Jesse A. — rosary maker

The Fire Didn't Touch Our Home

I've always had a personal devotion to the Rosary since childhood and am also a devotee of Our Lady of Fatima. March 14, 2025, seemed like a very normal day—I went to school, prayed my Rosaries and the Stations of the Cross, attended Mass, and went home.

That night, around 10 p.m., my family was already tucked into bed when we suddenly heard our neighbor shouting outside our fence. "FIRE! FIRE! FIRE!" The old, abandoned store directly behind our house had caught fire. This store is literally four or five feet from my bedroom window. We were all panicking.

Before leaving my room, I sprinkled holy water and left a small image of Our Lady of Fatima on my window, facing the direction of the fire. After moving out my important documents,

I also carried out my large images of Our Lady of Fatima and St. Joseph, entrusting our home to their protection.

The firefighters eventually managed to control the fire. Then my father called the hotline for the electricity company to ensure the safety of the power lines—and of all possible names, the dispatcher introduced herself as "Fatima." I took that as a signal grace from Our Lady herself. Despite the terrifying closeness of the fire, our house wasn't damaged at all. I will be forever devoted to the Rosary and Our Lady of Fatima!

Joseph Rodney A.—student

From Workaholic to Beloved Son

Even though I grew up praying the Rosary with my family, I didn't start praying it daily on my own until I came back to my faith in 2012. Back then, I was going through a dark and stressful period in my life and was desperate for change. I was a husband and father, and my wife and I were expecting twins. Work had become my idol, and I was a slave to it. There was no joy or freedom in it. So, I decided to pick up the rosary and try praying it on my way to work to see if it would help.

At first, I simply recited the prayers, often thinking about work the whole time. But just showing up each day to pray, even imperfectly, had a profound impact on my life and faith in the long run. My external world didn't change, but my heart, my disposition, and my perspective did. Mary led me through a purification process. I was able to slowly detach my identity from work, and more securely attach it to my true identity as a beloved son of the Father.

By 2016, I was so thoroughly convinced of the power of the Rosary that I turned my passion for woodworking into a Catholic rosary business as a means of spreading devotion to the Rosary. To this day, I credit Mary and the Rosary for being the reason I have a relationship with Christ.

Jonathan C.—husband, father, business owner

I Found My Mother on Mother's Day

When I was six, my parents divorced. At first, I stayed with my father, but eventually he had to work abroad, and I went to stay with my aunt and uncle in the countryside. I didn't have many rules to follow, except one that my aunt emphasized. She wrote down three prayers and placed them above the light switch in my room. The rule was simple: Every time I left the room, I had to stop and read the prayers—the Apostles' Creed, the Our Father, and the Hail Mary.

I remember feeling very sad when Mother's Day came around and the other children made cards for their moms. My aunt noticed my sadness and asked what was bothering me, and I told her. She was quiet for a moment before asking if I had been following the prayer rule. I said yes, and she asked me to say the prayers then and there. I did, and to my surprise, I had memorized them.

It was then that she said I was ready. She took me to her bedroom and let me choose a rosary from many she had. She told me I had a mother—Mary—who loves me and is always with me, even at that moment. This was when I was introduced to Mary and began learning about the Rosary. My aunt explained how each bead contained a treasure.

Now, in my mid-forties, I've never felt alone. In my darkest moments, as long as I can pray the Rosary, I know I have a mother who listens. My life has revolved around the Rosary, and it has been my lifesaver.

Gabriel L.—husband, photographer

I Couldn't Pray One, So I Prayed Four

I used to say, "I'm just not a Mary person," because it felt so boring and grueling when I tried to pray the Rosary.

Then I discovered the secret: Instead of praying one set of mysteries, I now pray all four! Praying four Rosaries a day crushed my idols and opened my heart to hear the voices of Jesus and Mary. I grew in patience, self-denial, obedience, and docility. The full Rosary even deepened my love for other devotions: Scripture, the Chaplet of Divine Mercy, and the sacraments.

The full Rosary helps you live in the Father's promise found in the Parable of the Prodigal Son: "Behold, you are with me always, and all that is mine is yours." If you want to "pray unceasingly," even when you're not praying the Rosary, pray all four mysteries daily.

Kim S. — pro-life advocate

"Give Mary One Week": Scrupulosity Healed

Growing up, I learned to pray the Rosary with my family on car rides. As I progressed to a daily Rosary on my own, I was tempted with lies to stop: I didn't have time, and I was praying them poorly anyway. You either give up the Rosary or you give up the sin; I gave up the Rosary, and in eighth/ninth grade I fell into sin. Then, when I went on a Catholic camp the summer before my sophomore year, I made an examination of conscience, and was determined to overcome that sin in particular. I confessed it, and never committed it again.

At that time, I had begun praying a daily Rosary, and God continued to draw me closer to Himself through the Rosary. Yet, I was still struggling with scrupulosity, which was the most emotional and mental pain I ever experienced. I heard a seminarian talking about the Rosary, saying, "Give me one week. Give Mary one week." I started praying four Rosaries every day, and about one week later my scrupulosity dramatically decreased.

Now, with the graces from the Rosary, I am even seriously discerning a vocation as a Carmelite nun! Praying four Rosaries a day has not only changed my life. The graces have flowed into the lives of those around me, and both of my parents now pray four Rosaries as well. The Rosary is so powerful, never be afraid of wasting your time with it.

Grace R. — student

RENEWING MY PRIESTLY LIFE

For many years, I prayed a Rosary per day (five mysteries) and was encouraged and strengthened by that devotion. Whenever I would renew my consecration to the Blessed Virgin Mary, I also found great renewal and I loved more, sinned less, and my ministry was more fruitful.

The way that I have felt drawn to live my consecration to Mary fully is by praying the full Rosary every day (twenty mysteries). At first, it seemed like a lot to think about, praying four sets of mysteries every day. However, I have found that it is easier to pray four than it is to pray one. Mary has shown me spiritual discipline and focus, rather than doing the minimal and hoping it works out at some point in the day.

My thoughts, rather than being drawn to low and earthly things throughout the day, are drawn to Jesus Christ and to the Blessed Virgin Mary. I am drawn to interceding for all those who are in need of God's grace. Peace rules in my soul, and Mary has given me a heart that burns with love for sinners as hers does. I am able to pray constantly for the people in my care through the Rosary and have seen conversions and miracles happening on a scale unknown to me before I began this devotion. I feel that this helps me to truly fulfill St. Paul's admonition to "pray without ceasing." Mary is teaching me how to make my whole life a living sacrifice of praise—as hers was.

Fr. Ben

The Cure that Doctors Couldn't Find

Since he was young, my child had a strange ailment in one part of his body. He would sometimes cry or hit himself in that area, and it concerned us deeply. But it came and went at unpredictable, random times, and the medical attention we sought yielded no answers at all.

During the lockdown of 2020, his ailment became more frequent and more intense. He was just ten years old at the time, and the ailment drove him mad with frustration, to the point where he threatened to "cut off" that part of his body. This terrified me. No doctors could offer an explanation, and I was at my wit's end—a mother going insane, watching her child suffer and feeling completely helpless.

I knew I needed help. I needed healing so that I could help my son. So I turned to Mother Mary.

I picked up the rosary and felt a prompting to pray the full Rosary, all the mysteries, spread throughout the day. It kept me sane while giving me peace. I prayed without knowing when the next "attack" would come—in a day, in a week, or two?

I kept going with my full Rosary, and before I knew it, a few months had passed with no episodes!

Five years have passed now, and it is clear—he has been cured. I have no doubt of Our Mother's intercession. Our Lady never fails us. Thank you, Mama!

Suzanne J.—mother

A Rosary of Grief and Loss

My spiritual journey with Mary and the Rosary took a huge leap when my five children and I were faced with the abrupt, terrible, earth-shattering loss of my husband. This loss involved not a "physical" death but the death of our marriage, family, and home. One day he was here, although battling a lot, and then one day he said he was leaving for good. The state of trauma we were all in was intense.

About six months after my husband left, a dear friend went on a pilgrimage and came home with a gift for me and my children—rosaries with a letter all about the power and the need to commit to praying the daily Rosary or even many Rosaries a day. We had always wanted to do this but never were disciplined enough, it seemed.

And yet here we are, two years later, still praying our daily Rosary at night. My children are comforted by the stability the Rosary provides at the end of chaotic days. The rhythm of the Rosary has not only borne abundant fruit in our prayer life, but it has also bonded and grounded us so beautifully. Our Lady has created this closeness in the six of us, and usually right after the Rosary, we are sharing about all sorts of things—the hard things, the suffering, the joyful things of family life.

Mary has been such a friend to me. I often envision myself conversing with her about my children. I believe my imagination has been reignited through the Rosary and mental prayer. I advocate for the overall health, truth, and goodness of my children and myself. I owe Our Lady our continuous healing, which we are so thankful for. To hear your fifteen-year-old son at the end of a long day, when I just need to get five kids to bed, stopping me to say, "Mom, the Rosary," brings me to tears.

I envision often our dear Mother in her power and glory stomping the head of the serpent. I know she is stomping out all the pressures that surround us and protecting us here in our home. I remember a time in my journey when the pain was so deep, the thoughts were so invasive, and a dear spiritual mentor told me to pray a Hail Mary each time they would come. The prayer of the Hail Mary reclaimed the thoughts and pain, moment by moment.

Miriam R. — mother, teacher

Every person who picks up the rosary and
prays it as a lifestyle has a story to tell. This
collection of testimonies is only a small sample
of the countless stories that exist across the
world. "If every one of them were written
down, I suppose that the world itself could not
contain the books that would be written."
— John 21:25

Endnotes

1   Catherine of Siena, Letter to Stefano Maconi (Letter 368), in
     The Letters of St. Catherine of Siena, vol. 4, ed. and trans. Suzanne
     Noffke (Tempe, AZ: Arizona Center for Medieval and Renaissance
     Studies, 2008).

2   St. Louis de Montfort, *The Secret of the Rosary* (New York: TAN
     Books, 1954), 105.

3   As quoted in Msgr. Joseph A. Cirrincione and Thomas A. Nelson,
     The Rosary and the Crisis of Faith: Fatima and World Peace (Char-
     lotte, NC: TAN Books, 1986), 34.

4   Jean Pierre Camus, *The Spirit of St. Francis de Sales*, trans. Ella
     McMahon (London: Burns and Oates, 1880), 221.

5   G. K. Chesterton, "Why I Am a Catholic," *Nash's Pall Mall Maga-
     zine*, September 1926, 63–69.

6   Pope Leo XIII, Encyclical Letter on the Rosary *Adiutricem* (Sep-
     tember 5, 1895), no. 24.

7   Athanasius of Alexandria, *On the Incarnation*, trans. and ed. John
     Behr (Yonkers, NY: St. Vladimir's Seminary Press, 2011), 54: 3.

8   St. Alphonsus Liguori, *Prayer: The Great Means of Salvation and
     Perfection*, ed. Rev. Eugene Grimm (Manchester, NH: Sophia
     Institute Press, 2021), 135.

9   Quoted in St. Alphonsus Liguori, *Prayer*, 132.

10   St. Francis de Sales, *An Introduction to the Devout Life*, trans. John
     Ryan (Charlotte, NC: TAN Books, 2010), 61.

11   St. Alphonsus Liguori, *The Glories of Mary* (Liguori, MO: Liguori Publications, 2000), 50.

12   St. Bernard of Clairvaux, *Homilia II super Missus est*, no. 17, *Patrologia Latina* 183:70–71.

13   St. Alphonsus Liguori, *Glories of Mary*, 96.

14   As quoted in Fr. Robert Fox, *The Intimate Life of Sister Lucia* (Fatima Family Apostolate, 2001), 315.

15   Bl. Jordan of Saxony, *Libellus de Principiis Ordinis Praedicatorum*, sec. 5.

16   Ibid., sec. 9.

17   As quoted in St. Louis de Montfort, *The Secret of the Rosary*, trans. Mary Barbour, T.O.P. (New York: TAN Books, 1954), 18–19.

18   St. Louis de Montfort, *Secret of the Rosary*, 62.

19   As quoted in St. Louis de Montfort, *Secret of the Rosary*, 62.

20   Second Vatican Council, Dogmatic Constitution on Divine Revelation *Dei Verbum* (November 18, 1965), no. 24.

21   St. Louis de Montfort, *Secret of the Rosary*, 45.

22   Ibid., 99.

23   Ibid., 24–25.

24   Ibid., 25.

25   As quoted in David Supple, O.S.B., *Virgin Wholly Marvelous: Praises of Our Lady by the Popes, Councils, Saints, and Doctors of the Church* (Cambridge, MA: Ravengate Press, 1991), 131.

26   St. Louis de Montfort, *Secret of the Rosary*, [A Red Rose, no. 4].

27   Ibid., [A Rosebud, no. 7].

28   Ibid., 29.

29   Ibid., 35.

30   Ibid., 125.

31   Abbé François Trochu, *Saint Bernadette Soubirous, 1844–1879,* trans. John Joyce, S.J. (Charlotte, NC: TAN Books, 2012), 43.

32   St. Maximilian Kolbe, *The Writings of St. Maximilian Maria Kolbe,* vol. 2, *Various Writings,* ed. Antonella Di Piazza (Lugano, Switzerland: Nerbini International, 2016), no. 1171.

33   Servant of God Lucia Dos Santos, *Fatima in Lucia's Own Words* (Fatima, Portugal: Secretariado Dos Pastorinhos, 2011), 11.

34   Ibid., 12.

35   Ibid., 108.

36   Quoted in "Sixth Apparition (October 13, 1917)," EWTN, https://www.ewtn.com/catholicism/devotions/sixth-apparition-of-our-lady-23368.

37   Quoted in Rory Michael Fox, *Saints, Popes and Blesseds Speak on the Rosary* (E-Saint Library, 2012), sec. 4.

38   George Weigel, *A Witness to Hope: The Biography of Pope John Paul II* (New York: Cliff Street Books, 1999), 28.

39   St. John Paul II, Angelus Message (October 29, 1978).

40   St. John Paul II, Apostolic Letter on the Most Holy Rosary *Rosarium Virginis Mariae* (October 16, 2002), no. 19.

41   Ibid., no. 8.

42   Quoted in Tomasz Szymczak, *Fonti Kolbiane III Conferenze — Processo* (Padua, Italy: Messaggero Di Sant'Antonio, 2023), 507.

43   Ingrid Solano, Nicholas R. Eaton, and K. Daniel O'Leary, "Pornography Consumption, Modality and Function in a Large Internet Sample," *Journal of Sex Research* 57, no. 1 (January 2020): 92–103.

44   St. Anthony Mary Claret, *Autobiography,* ed. Jose Maria Vinas, C.M.F (Chicago: Claretian Publications, 1976), 237.

45 Sr. Patricia Proctor, O.S.C., *101 Inspirational Stories of the Rosary* (Spokane, WA: Poor Clare Sisters, 2003), 51.

46 Pope St. John XXIII, "Radio Message for the Coronation of Our Lady of the Rosary of La Coruña, Spain" (Sept. 11, 1960).

47 Proctor, *101 Inspirational Stories of the Rosary*, 25.

48 Ávila quoted in St. Alphonsus Liguori, *Glories of Mary*, 330.

49 See Augusta Theodosia Drane, O.P., *The History of St. Dominic: Founder of the Friars Preachers* (London: Longmans, Green, 1891), 130.

50 St. Alphonsus Liguori, *Glories of Mary*, 368.

51 Ven. Fulton Sheen, *The World's First Love: Mary, Mother of God* (San Francisco: Ignatius Press, 1996), 211.

52 Servant of God John Hardon, "The Rosary: A Prayer for All Times, The Indispensable Prayer for Our Times," Real Presence Renewal, https://realpresencerenewal.org/primers/the-holy-rosary/.

53 St. Peter of Alcantara, *Treatise on Prayer and Meditation*, part 1.

54 St. John Paul II, *Rosarium Virgins Mariae*, no. 19.

55 Pope Benedict XVI, Recitation of the Holy Rosary Meditation, Pontifical Shrine of Pompeii (October 19, 2008).

56 St. Teresa of Jesus, *The Way of Perfection*, trans. a Discalced Carmelite (London: Baronius Press, 2005), 111.

57 Ávila quoted in Fr. Peter Thomas Rohrbach, *Conversation with Christ* (Charlotte, NC: TAN Books, 2012), 52.

58 As quoted in Rohrbach *Conversation with Christ*, 53.

59 St. Louis de Montfort, *Secret of the Rosary*, 106.

60 St. Alphonsus Liguori, *Prayer*, 136.

61 Ibid., 164.

62   St. John Bosco, *Forty Dreams of St. John Bosco: The Apostle of Youth*, trans. Thomas A. Judge (Rockford, IL: TAN Books, 1996), 416.

63   Pope Pius XI, Encyclical Letter on the Rosary *Ingravescentibus Malis* (September 29, 1937), no. 14.

64   As quoted in Liz Kelly, *The Rosary: A Path to Prayer* (Chicago, IL: Loyola Press, 2004), 86.

65   *Catechism of the Catholic Church*, 2nd ed. (Vatican City: Libreria Editrice Vaticana, 1997), no. 409.

66   As quoted in Pietro Tartaglia, *The Mysteries of the Rosary and Padre Pio* (San Giovani Rotondo, Italy: Our Lady of Grace Capuchin Friary, 1999), 106.

67   Diane Montagna, "Cardinal Caffarra: 'What Sr. Lucia Wrote to Me Is Being Fulfilled Today,'" *Aleteia*, May 19, 2017 https://aleteia.org/2017/05/19/exclusive-cardinal-caffarra-what-sr-lucia-wrote-to-me-is-being-fulfilled-today/.

68   Weigel, *Witness to Hope*, 4.

69   St. Louis-Marie Grignion de Montfort, *True Devotion to Mary, with Preparation for Total Consecration*, trans. Fathers of the Company of Mary (Charlotte, NC: TAN Books, 2010), 110.

70   St. Maximilian M. Kolbe, *The Kolbe Reader*, ed. Anselm W. Romb, O.F.M. Conv. (Libertyville, IL: Marytown Press, 1987), 1071.

71   *Catechism of the Catholic Church*, no. 1776, quoting *Gaudium et Spes*, no. 16.

72   St. Josemaría Escrivá, *Furrow* (New York: Scepter Press, 1986), 265.

73   Jean-Baptiste Chautard, *The Soul of the Apostolate* (Rockford, IL: TAN Books, 2008), 41.

74   Quoted in Ray Sullivan, "The Wisdom of a Super-Saint, St. John Vianney," *Catholic Stand*, April 18, 2022, https://catholicstand.com/the-wisdom-of-a-super-saint-st-john-vianney/.

75   As quoted in Cirrincione and Nelson, *The Rosary and the Crisis of Faith*, 32.

76   Pope St. John Paul II, Message to the Bishop of Leiria-Fátima for the 80th Anniversary of the Fátima Apparitions (October 1, 1997).

77   J. R. R. Tolkien, *The Two Towers* (Boston: William Morrow, 2015), 506.

78   St. Louis de Montfort, *Secret of the Rosary*, 10.

79   As quoted in St. Louis de Montfort, *Secret of the Rosary*, 80.

80   *Catechism of the Catholic Church*, no. 1302.

81   St. Louis-Marie Grignion de Montfort, *True Devotion to Mary*, 15.

82   As quoted in Ann M. Brown, *Apostle of the Rosary: Blessed Bartolo Longo* (New Hope, KY: New Hope Publications, 2004), 53.

83   St. Maria Faustina Kowalska, *Diary of Saint Maria Faustina Kowalska: Divine Mercy in My Soul*, trans. Helena M. Pyzalski (Stockbridge, MA: Marian Press, 2012), no. 961.

84   Servant of God Joseph Kentenich, *Mary, Our Mother and Educator: An Applied Mariology* (Waukesha, WI: Schoenstatt Sisters of Mercy, 1987), 11.

85   St. Maximilian Maria Kolbe, *The Writings of St. Maximilian Maria Kolbe*, no. 1334.

86   Ibid., no. 980.

87   Fr. Benedict J. Groeschel, "Letter to Father Lawrence T. Picachy, S. J., February 13, 1963" in *The Rosary: Chain of Hope* (San Francisco: Ignatius Press, 2003), 16.

88   St. Maximilian Kolbe, *The Writings of St. Maximilian Maria Kolbe*, no. 1117.

89   Pope St. Paul VI, Encyclical Letter on Prayers for Peace *Christi Matri* (September 15, 1966), no. 10.

90   As quoted in Gabriel Harty, O.P., *The Rosary: The History of the Heart* (Dundalk, Ireland: Dundalgan Press, 2015), 29.

91   Pope Leo XIII, Encyclical Letter on the Rosary *Magnae Dei Matris* (September 8, 1892), no. 18.

92   St. Louis de Montfort, *Secret of the Rosary*, 12–13.

93   Bl. Gabriele Allegra, *Mary's Immaculate Heart: A Way to God* (Chicago: Franciscan Herald Press, 1985), 54.

94   St. John Bosco, *The Life of Saint Dominic Savio*, trans. Paul Aronica (New Rochelle, NY: Salesiana Publishers, 1963), 118.

95   Bl. James Alberione, *Mary, Queen of Apostles* (Boston: Daughters of St. Paul, 1976), 264.

96   St. Maria Faustina Kowalska, *Diary: Divine Mercy in My Soul*, 20.

97   As quoted in Catherine Moran, *Praying the Rosary with the Saints*, E-reader version, 2013.

98   St. Louis-Marie Grignion de Montfort, *True Devotion to Mary*, 19.

99   St. Maximilian Maria Kolbe, *The Writings of St. Maximilian Maria Kolbe*, no. 987b.

100   St. Louis de Montfort, *Secret of the Rosary*, 31.

101   Thomas Aquinas, *Summa Theologiae*, III, q. 40, art. 3.

102   St. John Eudes, *The Admirable Heart of Mary*, trans. Fr. J. M. Debussi (New York: P. J. Kenedy & Sons, 1948), 206.

103   As quoted in Passionist Sisters, *Prayers to St. Gabriel* (Erlanger, KY: Passionist Nuns Monastery 2012), 3.

104   St. Alphonsus Liguori, *Glories of Mary*, 127.

105   Sheen, *World's First Love*, 214.

106   Ibid., 213.

107   Ibid., 214–215.

108 St. Josemaría Escrivá, *Furrow*, 186.

109 As quoted in Jeanne Gosselin Arnold, *A Man of Faith: Father Patrick Peyton, C. S. C., His Life, Mission, and Message* (Hollywood, CA: Family Theater, 1983), 250.

110 As quoted in Arnold, *A Man of Faith*, 202.

111 As quoted in Arnold, *A Man of Faith*, 34.

112 As quoted in Cirrincione and Nelson, *The Rosary and the Crisis of Faith*, 33.

113 Ven. Patrick Peyton, *All for Her* (Hollywood, CA: Family Theater Productions, 1973), 1.

114 St. John Paul II, *Rosarium Virginis Mariae*, no. 41.

115 As quoted in Fr. Willy Raymond, C.S.C., "Mary, the Pope, and the American Apostle of the Family Rosary," in *Behold Your Mother: Priests Speak about Mary*, ed. Stephen J. Rossetti (Notre Dame, IN: Ave Maria Press, 2007), 52.

116 As quoted in Deacon Andrew J. Gerakas, *The Rosary and Devotion to Mary* (Boston: St. Paul Books & Media, 1992), 76.

117 As quoted in Raymond, "Mary, the Pope, and the American Apostle," 53.

118 Pope Pius XI, *Ingravescentibus Malis*, 28.

119 As quoted in Arnold, *A Man of Faith*, 250.

120 Pope Benedict XVI, General Audience (October 26, 2005).

121 St. Anthony Mary Claret, *El Colegial Ó Seminarista Teórica y Prácticamente Instruido: Tome I* (Barcelona, Spain: Librería Religiosa, 1861), 279.

122 As quoted in Fr. Matthias M. Sasko, F.I., *Preparation for Total Consecration to the Immaculate: According to St. Maximilian M. Kolbe* (New Bedford, MA: Academy of the Immaculate, 2023), 78.

123 As quoted in Brown, *Apostle of the Rosary*, 43.

124 Sheen, *World's First Love*, 215.

125 St. Louis-Marie Grignion de Montfort, *True Devotion to Mary*, 21–25.

Sophia Institute

Sophia Institute is a nonprofit institution that seeks to nurture the spiritual, moral, and cultural life of souls and to spread the gospel of Christ in conformity with the authentic teachings of the Roman Catholic Church.

Sophia Institute Press fulfills this mission by offering translations, reprints, and new publications that afford readers a rich source of the enduring wisdom of mankind.

Sophia Institute also operates the popular online resource CatholicExchange.com. *Catholic Exchange* provides world news from a Catholic perspective as well as daily devotionals and articles that will help readers to grow in holiness and live a life consistent with the teachings of the Church.

In 2013, Sophia Institute launched Sophia Institute for Teachers to renew and rebuild Catholic culture through service to Catholic education. With the goal of nurturing the spiritual, moral, and cultural life of souls, and an abiding respect for the role and work of teachers, we strive to provide materials and programs that are at once enlightening to the mind and ennobling to the heart; faithful and complete, as well as useful and practical.

Sophia Institute gratefully recognizes the Solidarity Association for preserving and encouraging the growth of our apostolate over the course of many years. Without their generous and timely support, this book would not be in your hands.

www.SophiaInstitute.com
www.CatholicExchange.com
www.SophiaTeachers.org

Sophia Institute Press is a registered trademark of Sophia Institute.
Sophia Institute is a tax-exempt institution as defined by the
Internal Revenue Code, Section 501(c)(3). Tax ID 22-2548708.